# The Calico House

## Joanna Brazier

# CREDITS

Editor-in-Chief . . . . . . . . . . . . . . .Barbara Weiland
Technical Editor . . . . . . . . . . . . . . Kerry I. Hoffman
Managing Editor . . . . . . . . . . . . . . . . . Greg Sharp
Copy Editor . . . . . . . . . . . . . . . . . . Liz McGehee
Proofreader . . . . . . . . . . . . . . . . . Leslie Phillips
Design Director . . . . . . . . . . . . . . . . .Judy Petry
Text and Cover Design . . . . . . . . Joanne Lauterjung
Production Assistant . . . . . . . . . Claudia L'Heureux
Illustrators . . . . . . . . . . . . . . . . . . . Laurel Strand
Stephanie Benson
Illustration Assistant . . . . . . . . . . . .Lisa McKenney
Cover Illustration . . . . . . . . . . . . Sandra Seligmiller
Title Page Illustration . . . . . . . . . . . . . . .Ian Warne
Photography . . . . . . . . . . . . . . . . . . .Bill Shaylor
Art Direction and Photo Styling . . . . Joanna Brazier

The Calico House
© 1995 by Joanna Brazier
That Patchwork Place, Inc., PO Box 118, Bothell, WA
98041-0118 USA

Printed in Hong Kong
00 99 98 97 96 95    6 5 4 3 2 1

**Library of Congress Cataloging-in-Publication Data**
Brazier, Joanna,
   The Calico House : Perth, Western Australia / Joanna Brazier.
      p.    cm. — (International quilt shop series)
   ISBN 1-56477-093-1 (pbk.)
   1. Calico House (Perth, W.A.) 2. Patchwork—Australia—Patterns. 3. Quilting—Australia—Patterns. 4. Quilts—Australia.
I. Title. II. Series.
TT835.B67 1995
746.46—dc20                                        95-892
                                                          CIP

# DEDICATION

*To my parents, who physically departed far too early but left me with the strength to survive. My mother, for her values, work ethic, good colour sense, and tidiness! My father, for the desire to dream.*

# ACKNOWLEDGMENTS

*With great appreciation and many thanks to:*

*My marvellous staff, who are actually more like family—much valued and loved;*

*My beautiful daughter, Sarah, who has believed in me since day one of "The Calico House" and knows how hard it has often been;*

*My loyal husband, John, who is understanding and supportive and tries very hard to make me heed stock controls;*

*Our customers, many of whom we have come to call our friends;*

*Hilda, for the laughs we had while mastering the computer—what a team;*

*Anne Bloemen, for her positive comments and proofreading;*

*Bill Shaylor, for his patience and easy manner, and for his photography that presents us in such a good light;*

*Kerry Hoffman, my editor at That Patchwork Place, for her friendly assistance from a distance;*

*And finally, Nancy J. Martin and Barbara Weiland, for inviting us to share our store "down under" with the world.*

## MISSION STATEMENT

WE ARE DEDICATED TO PROVIDING QUALITY PRODUCTS THAT ENCOURAGE CREATIVITY AND PROMOTE SELF-ESTEEM IN OUR CUSTOMERS AND OUR EMPLOYEES.

WE STRIVE TO MAKE A DIFFERENCE IN THE LIVES WE TOUCH.

*That Patchwork Place is an employee-owned, financially secure company.*

# Contents

AUSTRALIA HAS 700 DIFFERENT KINDS OF BIRDS,
12,000 SPECIES OF FLOWERING PLANTS,
AND ABOUT 230 SPECIES OF MAMMALS.
SOME OF ITS UNUSUAL ANIMALS ARE THE KOALA,
KANGAROO, PLATYPUS, DINGO, AND WOMBAT.

PHOTO BY BETTY METZ.

# Introduction

THE CALICO HOUSE

When I was asked to join That Patchwork Place's International Quilt Shop Series, I was thrilled, but a little daunted. Perth is one of the most isolated cities in the world with a relatively small population. Could I put together a book that would be of interest to readers everywhere? Writing many newsletters over the years was one thing, but a book! Oh well, I had always wanted to be an author. Besides, quilt shop owners are known devils for punishment and well used to meeting challenges head on.

The Calico House staff and teachers all rose to the challenge to help. I hope you enjoy the quilts that we have shared with you and that you will "join us for morning tea" by making some of the sweet treats that are very Australian. The "Aussie Snippets" that we have scattered throughout the book might tempt you just enough to make plans to visit Australia—and us!

Although we are a long way from anywhere, we would love for you to visit us if you ever make it "down under." Or, write and tell us about your part of the world. We would be thrilled to receive a photo of anything you might make from our book! Find our address under "Resources" on page 92.

Now, on with our story . . .

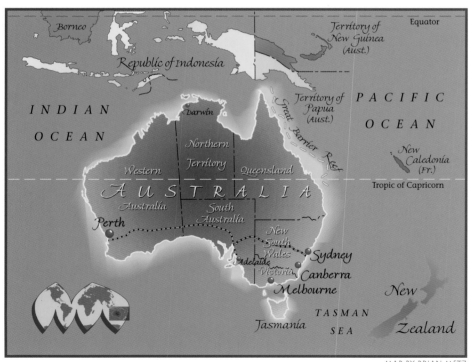

MAP BY BRIAN METZ.

*As you enter the Calico House, the friendly staff are waiting to help you! Jenny Burke (left) and Jan Tocas are my longest-serving employees and have become dear and loyal friends.*

Twelve years ago, I found myself single again with a ten-year-old daughter, a dog and a cat, and no real career, except for a few years in an interior-decorating partnership with a friend. With a growing interest in colour and design and the obvious need for a craft shop in our area, I started to pursue the idea of opening my own shop.

First, I enrolled in a night course in small-business ownership at the University of Western Australia. I will always remember the words of our lecturer on the first night after asking how many of us were about to open a business. We all raised our hands. "Seventy percent of you will fail in the first two years," he went on to say. With these words ringing in my ears, my next mission was to convince the local—and extremely conservative—bank manager that I was worthy of a very small loan. He was dubious to say the least and not keen on the combined "risk" that I was a single mother venturing into a new business.

Pressing on, I found premises that were old and large and showed potential. All that was needed was some loving attention to bring it all to life—and a bucket or two of blood, sweat, and tears!

Under the dreadful carpet, wonderful jarrah floorboards were just waiting to be polished once more, and the three big storefront windows were calling out to be "dressed" to face the street. Taking a deep breath, we opened our doors in July 1983.

The fabric stock then consisted of a few rolls of pretty little prints to suit the "cottage craft" enthusiasts who used them to line baskets, cover tissue boxes, and make padded photo frames. After a year and a half, I focused on buying a larger variety of fabrics and developing quilt classes.

Most of my first employees are still with me, and we often laugh about those early days of learning by experience. Often, I would teach two classes during the day and then return again at night to conduct another class. My daughter, Sarah, would come with me and do her homework at the end of the table. I pinch myself now as I recall raising a child, running a shop, and renovating a house all at the same time. Did it really happen? This is the stuff quilt shop owners need to be made of—plus a streak of masochism and a dose of madness thrown in for good measure!

*The ribbon cupboard looks so inviting.*

Etched in my mind is the memory of my first trip to the annual International Quilt Market in Houston, Texas, a 30-hour flight away. It was overwhelming and exciting. I wanted to ship all of those wonderful wares to Australia. It took months for things to appear on The Calico House shelves because of the long sea voyage. I don't think I slept more than a few hours all week as my mind raced with new ideas for merchandise and classes.

Now, I try to attend one Quilt Market a year, as there is, unfortunately, a lack of local stock made in Australia. Fabric, books, ribbons, and many of the notions still have to be imported from overseas.

As you know, purchasing material becomes addictive, and shop owners are not immune! We now stock over 2,000 bolts of fabric in almost every colourway and design, with the only limitation being space and that boring factor of life, the BUDGET.

The standard and quality of work in Australia is extremely high in the quilting, embroidery, smocking, and general craft areas. We believe we have helped contribute to this creative growth by providing the latest stock available, introducing new ideas, holding many classes and workshops, and just by be-

lieving in the importance of craft, in all its forms, in people's lives. Our classes try to provide the knowledge and stimulation for students to develop their skills and find their inner creativity. This is a most satisfying aspect of the business. Quite often, former students go on to become excellent teachers as they gain confidence and want to share their ideas.

We love the little notes that often accompany mail orders. Recently one lady wrote, "from under my gum tree" and another told me in dramatic detail of a frightening day when a poisonous snake lay at her front door! One customer lives in an underground cave house in the opal mining fields of Coober Pedy in South Australia, and our parcels help her keep in touch with the "outside world."

I like to think The Calico House provides a pleasurable place to contemplate the next quilt or seek inspiration for other craft projects or home-decorating ideas. Three years ago, our lease expired and we went through the upheaval of moving the shop. We all survived and The Calico House continues—bigger and brighter. Over the last decade, customers, students, staff, and I have all grown and benefited from being part of the wonderful world of quilting.

# Meet the Staff

Someone once said, "A business is only as good as its people," and the members of The Calico House staff are a great bunch of people. As they are all keen stitchers, they are happy to assist with projects and provide creative help and ideas.

*The Calico House staff with the beautiful Swan River behind them. Back row (from left): Lynette LeRoy and Sarah Barker (my daughter). Middle row: Jan Tocas, Melodie Slatter, Susan Readhead, and Jan Houghton. Front row: Jenny Burke, Joanna Brazier (with Mini, my dachshund), Jan Mullen, and Hilda Klass.*

# The Calico House Album

What would a quilt shop be without its customers, or a quilt class be without its students? One of the most rewarding aspects of being involved in the world of handcrafts is that your customers often become your friends.

We have been treated to farm-fresh eggs, homemade jam, champagne, and chocolates at Christmas. We have even been presented with a basket full of coloured eggs at Easter. But more important, we also receive blessings and prayers when someone is ill, and we cherish the gift of friendship from our favourite customers.

Quilters are a caring and sharing group of people. "Reach for the Stars" is a quilt that was made for the Immuno-Deficiency Ward at Royal Perth Hospital in 1994 by (from the front, counter-clockwise) Jan Mullen, Helen Ryan, Wendy Sier, Jan Houghton, Jenny Burke, Jan Tocas, Hilda Klass, Melodie Slatter, Judy Campbell, and Susan Readhead.

Nancy Harrison, with quilts and bears made in classes at The Calico House. Nancy has been kind enough to let us visit her at her delightful farm in Margaret River, 174 miles from Perth.

with strong interest in cross-stitch and teddy bears, we have begun our own clubs. Hilda Klass (left) is an enthusiastic cross-stitcher, who happily shares her skills. Lynette LeRoy is a devoted arctophile (friend of teddy bears), who designs her own bear patterns for club members and the shop.

The Calico House smocking teacher, Margaret Herzfeld (standing), with Wilma Derickx (left) and Moira Schneider.

Quilt shops always need new ideas for classes and display items to dress windows. Susan Readhead (left) and Jan Mullen are constantly creating exciting new quilts that make my job easier. Such clever girls!

who says quilts and bills don't mix? Our bookkeeper, Diana Simpson, often puts down her pen and gives us a hug when we look like we need it! Plus, she doesn't nag me about my addiction for purchasing even more fabric when the shelves are already full!

Our resident patchwork teacher, Wendy Sier (standing right), with Fay Schorer, and seated (left to right): Jo Kitts, Cheryl Babich, and Val York.

# Coming Up Roses

Coming Up Roses, designed by Joanna Brazier and Jan Mullen, 1994,
Perth, Western Australia, 68" x 84". Machine quilted by Jan Mullen.

Closeup detail of lower right corner of "Coming Up Roses" quilt,
showing small and large squares.

*ow I love pink roses—all roses, really—but especially pink. Every event in my life, both happy and sad, has been made more memorable by the presence and perfume of pink roses. My favourites range from little darling Cecile Brunner rosebuds, to the beautiful full buds of First Love and Michelle Meilland, to the soft blooms of David Austin's old-fashioned and sweet-smelling delights.*

*Twice I have visited Monet's garden in Giverny, France, and have felt that heaven must be just like this. A delightful pink house, a yellow dining room, a blue-and-white kitchen, and a garden to die for. All things I love, especially his pink roses—Albertine, Eva, and Constance Spry.*

*Claude Monet said, "More than anything, I must have flowers, always, always..."*

*The quilt is my tribute to Monet. It is made with squares cut from all the softly toned rose fabrics in the shop at the time. The first quilt I made for my daughter was pretty squares of fabric sewn together and I still like the simplicity and symmetry of this design.*

*Perhaps you have a theme of your own. Choose from the fabulous array of fabrics available today—sunflowers, pansies, or even cows or chickens! It gives us another excuse to hunt for fabric—as if we needed a reason!*

*On the steps leading to Monet's home—a little bit of heaven. Giverny, France, 1993.*

## MATERIALS: *44"-wide fabric*

6 yds. assorted large-scale floral prints*
2⅛ yds. solid for inner border
½ yd. for binding
5 yds. for backing
71" x 86" piece of batting

*\*Yardage is difficult to estimate as roses are cut from the fabrics, leaving plenty of scraps for future projects. The more fabrics you have to work with, the better. If you want to make this quilt without regard to centring roses in each square, five yards are required.*

## CUTTING

Place masking tape on the corner of your Bias Square® to mark the size square to cut and to use as a window template to help you centre the flowers in each square. Mark a 4½" square for centre panel and outer border squares. Mark a 1½" square for the pieced inner border squares.

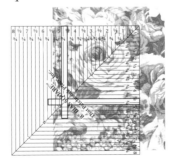

*From the assorted floral prints, cut:*
301 squares, each 4½" x 4½", for centre panel and outer border
500 squares, each 1½" x 1½", for pieced inner border

## Helpful Hints

*To help regulate the design while you are arranging the squares, divide them into a "large print" group and a "small print" group. Alternating the placement of each gives order to the design.*

*From solid inner border fabric, cut:*
8 strips, each 1½" x 72", along the lengthwise grain

## ASSEMBLING THE QUILT TOP

1. Arrange the 4½" squares in a pleasing way to form the centre panel and the 4 border units. Leave a gap for addition of the inner borders.

   Centre panel: 11 vertical rows of 15 squares each
   Outer side border units: 2 vertical rows of 17 squares each
   Outer top and bottom border units: 2 rows of 17 squares each

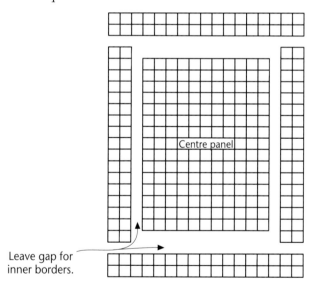

Leave gap for inner borders.

2. Use chain-piecing techniques to stitch the squares together in vertical rows. (See page 83.)
3. Arrange the 1½" squares in a pleasing way to form the 4 pieced inner border strips.

   Side border strips: 2 vertical rows of 70 squares each
   Top and bottom border strips: 2 rows of 55 squares each

4. Use chain-piecing techniques to stitch the squares together into rows.

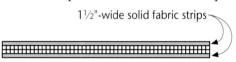

Top and Bottom Inner Border Units
Make 2.

Side Inner Border Units
Make 2.

5. Measure each of the pieced inner border strips. Trim the 1½"-wide solid fabric strips to match the measurements. Sew a solid fabric strip to the long sides of the 4 pieced inner border strips.

1½"-wide solid fabric strips

6. Attach the resulting border units to the centre panel, following the directions on pages 87–88 for mitred borders.
7. Sew the side outer borders to the quilt top first, following the directions on pages 86–87 for borders with straight-cut corners. Sew the top and bottom outer borders in place. Press the seams towards the inner border.

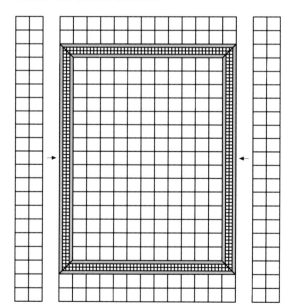

## FINISHING THE QUILT

1. Layer the quilt top with batting and backing; baste.
2. Quilt as desired.
3. Bind the edges with 2½"-wide strips cut from the crosswise grain of your binding fabric. (See pages 90–91.)

# Alexandra's Toy Shelf

*Isn't it special when we can toss challenges to people, knowing they will understand the concept and then rise to the occasion and produce something just like you hoped for—or even better?*

*Susan Readhead is one of those creative people. Under the trying circumstances of building a home, Susan completed this toy quilt in limited time and named it for her daughter, Alexandra.*

*We all think this quilt is delightful and just know it will give much pleasure to any child. Perhaps, you will want to replace Alexandra's toys with your child's favourites!*

*Alexandra's Toy Shelf by Susan Readhead, 1994, Perth, Western Australia, 31½" x 43".*

## MATERIALS: *44"-wide fabric*

½ yd. brown print for shelves
1 yd. light solid for background
¼ yd. each assorted solids and prints for toys*
1 yd. medium print for border and binding
1½ yds. for backing (if cut across width of fabric)
36" x 46" piece of batting
Assorted ribbons, yarn, gathered cotton lace,
    tapestry wool, and a bell (See step 7, page 15.)
Embroidery threads
Template plastic or freezer paper for appliqué

*When you are selecting fabrics for the toys, try to picture each toy as a whole and choose the fabric best suited for it. Balance the colours, patterns, light and dark values, and solid and printed fabrics. Contrast is very important. To add variety, place directional fabrics like plaids, checks, and stripes on the bias.*

## CUTTING

*All strips are cut from the crosswise grain of the fabric.*

*From the brown fabric, cut:*
3 strips, each 1½" x 23½", for shelves
2 strips, each 1½" x 31½"; crosscut into 6 strips, each
    1½" x 10½", for sides of toy shelves
1 strip, 5½" x 23½", for decorative shelf top

*From the light background fabric, cut:*
3 strips, each 10½" x 21½", for the shelf background
    panels

*From the border fabric, cut:*
1 strip, 6" x 23½", for top border
1 strip, 4½" x 23½", for bottom border
2 strips, each 4½" x 43", for side borders
4 strips, each 3" x 43", for binding (You may need to
    cut an additional strip for the binding, after you
    have measured your completed quilt.)

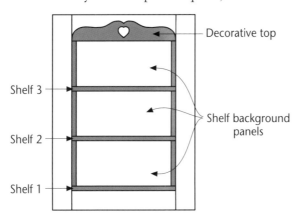

## ASSEMBLING THE QUILT TOP

*Use ¼"-wide seam allowances. Since some of the toys are draped over the shelves, it is necessary to complete the shelf framework before appliquéing the toys in place.*

1. With right sides together, stitch a 1½" x 10½" brown strip to each short side of a 10½" x 21½" shelf background panel. Press the seam towards the brown strip. Repeat with the remaining 2 background panels.

Make 3.

2. With right sides together, stitch a 1½" x 23½" brown strip to 1 long side of each of the shelf background panels. Press seams towards the brown strip.

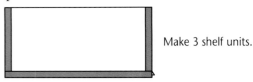

Make 3 shelf units.

3. Sew the 3 shelf units together as shown. Press seams towards the brown strip.

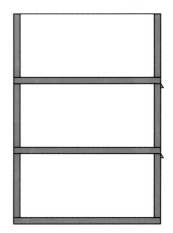

4. Prepare the top border, which includes the decorative shelf top. Make a plastic template (see page 84) for the decorative shelf top, using the pattern on the pullout pattern insert. Trace the design onto the right side of the 5½" x 23½" brown strip. Cut out the fabric piece, adding a ¼"-wide seam allowance all around. Be sure to add the same seam allowance to the heart shape.

    Lay the decorative cutout piece on top of the top border strip, so that the right side of each piece faces up. Align the bottom raw edges and baste the two pieces together, about ⅛" inside the bottom edge as shown. The curved edge of the decorative shelf top will be appliquéd later.

5. Sew the top and bottom borders in place. Add the side borders, measuring and cutting as directed for borders with straight-cut corners on page 86.

Appliqué curved edge later. —

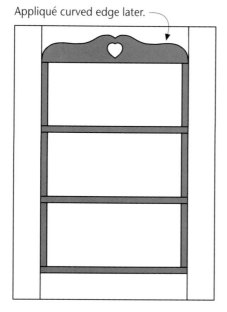

Your shelves are now ready for the toys!

## APPLIQUÉ

*Patterns for the toys are on the pullout pattern insert. Note that patterns are reversed. Appliqué the pieces for each toy in the numerical order indicated on the patterns. Appliqué techniques begin on page 84.*

1. Make plastic templates of the toys. If you prefer, make freezer-paper templates instead. See "Making Templates" on page 84 and "Freezer-Paper Appliqué" on page 85.
2. Refer to the colour photo for placement of the toys on the shelves. Using a marking pencil, trace the outline of each toy onto your background. The pencil marks will be your guide for placement of each piece.
3. Trace around each template onto the right side of the appliqué fabric. Cut out the appliqué pieces, adding a scant ¼"-wide (³⁄₁₆" to ¼") seam allowance around all pieces.
4. Pin the appliqué pieces in place, aligning them with the drawn placement lines.

*NOTE:* Some appliqué pieces are layered on top of others. Do not turn under seam allowances that will be covered by other appliqué pieces.

5. Appliqué each toy in place. Always use thread to match the appliqué piece, not the background fabric. Use the method of appliqué that you prefer.
6. Appliqué the curved edge of the decorative shelf top.
7. Next, add embroidery stitches and embellishments to personalize your quilt. Embroidery stitches are indicated on the patterns. Refer to the embroidery stitches on page 89. Add the following embellishments.

  • Tie a 12" length of ¾"-wide ribbon in a bow around Edward Bear's neck.
  • Centre 2" long pieces of yarn on the edge of the Doll's head and stitch in place by machine as shown.

  • Add a 4" length of cotton lace ruffle to the Doll's dress collar; add a 1½" length to each Doll's sleeve.
  • Add a 3" length of ¼"-wide ribbon for the Sailor Boy's hatband.
  • Tie a 3" length of ¼"-wide ribbon in a knot for the Sailor Boy's tie.
  • Stitch a 3" length of ribbon around the Bear's neck for a collar.
  • Stitch bell to the tip of the Jack-in-the-Box cap.
  • Pleat a 6" length of ½"-wide ribbon and stitch in place for the Jack-in-the-Box collar; pleat 3" lengths and stitch in place for the cuffs.
  • Using tapestry wool, embroider the buttons on the Jack-in-the-Box with large French knots.

## FINISHING THE QUILT

1. Layer the quilt top with batting and backing; baste.
2. Quilt as desired. Refer to "Marking the Quilting Design" on page 88. Susan outline-quilted ¼" inside the shelves and crosshatched the background.
3. Bind the edges with 3"-wide straight-grain strips of the medium print. (See pages 90–91.)

*Light & Shade Liberty by Judy Turner, 1994, Canberra, ACT, Australia, 34½" x 45½".*

WILDFLOWERS THAT BLOOM AROUND PERTH IN SPRING. PHOTO BY PHOTO INDEX.

The quilt-as-you-go wall hanging on page 16 looks wonderful in its shades of light and dark. It's an ideal way to use treasured Liberty of London™ scraps as well as new Liberty fabric. If you have fabric samples, use them in the corners of the blocks. Don't forget that if a fabric has too much contrast or is too dark, turn the fabric over and use the reverse side. To gain a light and shade effect without a striped appearance, blend the fabrics within each block.

Judy has collected one hundred different Liberty fabrics over the years, and she wanted to keep the design simple to show them off.

Judy began quiltmaking in 1981 and has been blending printed fabrics since 1983. Her strongest influence has been her mother, and she also credits Claude Monet, Kaffe Fasset, Fred Williams, Deirdre Amsden, and Grace Earl as sources of inspiration.

## MATERIALS: 44"-wide fabric

1½ yds. assorted light prints for blocks*
1½ yds. assorted dark prints for blocks*
1⅓ yds. dark print for binding and seam-covering strips
2¼ yds. for backing
38" x 49" piece of thin batting

*If you use Liberty fabrics, which are 36" wide, you will need 2 yards each of light and dark prints.

## CUTTING

From the crosswise grain of each of the light and dark prints for blocks, cut a selection of strips, varying the widths from 1" to 2½" wide. As you stitch the strips together, you will cut more strips to achieve a blended look.

From the backing fabric, cut:
11 strips, each 5" x 42"; crosscut into 82 squares, each 5" x 5", for square blocks
2 strips, each 6" x 42"; crosscut into 14 squares, each 6" x 6", for triangle blocks

From the batting, cut:
9 strips, each 5" x 49"; crosscut into 82 squares, each 5" x 5", for square blocks
2 strips, each 6" x 49"; crosscut into 14 squares, each 6" x 6", for triangle blocks

From the lengthwise grain of the binding/seam-covering fabric, cut:
2 strips, each 4" x 48", for binding
2 strips, each 4" x 36", for binding
13 strips, each 1" x 48", for seam-covering strips on back of quilt

# MAKING THE BLOCKS

*Use ¼"-wide seam allowances. Read all of the directions carefully before beginning.*

## Square Blocks

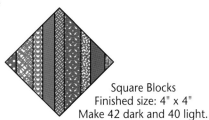

Square Blocks
Finished size: 4" x 4"
Make 42 dark and 40 light.

1. Pin the 5" squares of batting to the 5" squares of backing fabric.
2. Lay the first fabric strip diagonally across the centre of the block as shown.

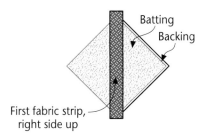

Batting
Backing

First fabric strip,
right side up

3. Place the second strip right sides together on top of the first strip, aligning the raw edges. Allow enough fabric to cover the batting, when the strip is flipped onto the batting. Pin in place. Stitch the strips together through all the layers. Flip the second strip over the batting and finger-press. Add the next strip in the same manner. Continue until that side of the square is covered with strips. Repeat with the other side of the square until the square is completely covered. Cover 42 of the 5" squares with dark fabric strips and 40 with light fabric strips. Blend the colors as you add strips. You may need to cut more fabric strips as you work.

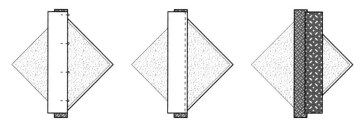

4. Trim each block to 4½" x 4½". Use a Bias Square® ruler to trim the blocks. Make sure the diagonal line (45° angle) of the ruler is parallel with the seam lines that join the fabric strips. You can make a cutting template if you prefer. Refer to "Squaring Up the Blocks" on page 86.

## Triangle Blocks

Triangle Blocks
Make 12 dark and 16 light.

1. Pin the 6" squares of batting to the 6" squares of backing fabric.
2. Cover 6 of the squares with dark strips and 8 with light strips in the same manner as you did in step 3 of the square blocks.
3. Trim each block to 5" x 5" as you did for the 4½" x 4½" squares. Cut the squares in half through the centre diagonally, parallel to the strips.

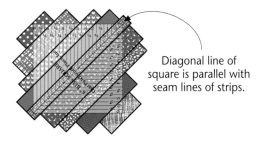

Diagonal line of
square is parallel with
seam lines of strips.

# ASSEMBLING THE QUILT TOP

***NOTE:*** Measure the length of long seam-covering strips as you go, so the remainder of the strip can be used where short pieces are needed.

1. Arrange the light and dark square and triangle blocks as shown in the photo on page 16.
2. Referring to the Assembly Sequence Plan and beginning in the top right-hand corner of the quilt (Diagonal Row 1), pin T1 (dark triangle) to T2 (light triangle), with the quilt-top sides together as shown. Remember: the backing fabric is the same for all of the blocks! Pin a length of the 1"-wide seam-covering strip in place with the right side of the covering strip facing the backing of T2. Align the raw edges of the triangles with the raw edge of the covering strip. Stitch the seam and strip together. Trim the seam allowances slightly to reduce the bulk where the blocks meet. Fold the strip to cover the raw edges of the seam, turn under a ¼"-wide seam allowance, and blindstitch in place.

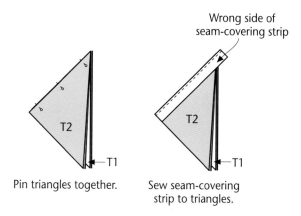

Pin triangles together.

Sew seam-covering strip to triangles.

Wrong side of seam-covering strip

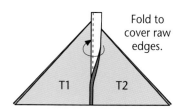

Fold to cover raw edges.

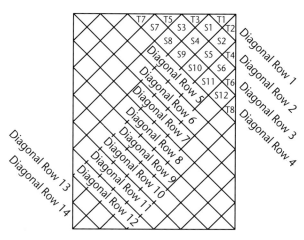

Assembly Sequence Plan

3. Repeat the same process and stitch together the squares and triangles in each of the remaining diagonal rows. Make sure you always sew the seam-covering strips on the same side when joining the pieces so the grid formed on the back will line up when the diagonal rows are joined.

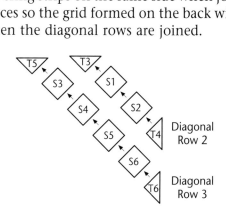

Diagonal Row 2

Diagonal Row 3

4. Pin diagonal rows 1 and 2 together, then pin a length of seam-covering strip in place as you did when you joined squares together. Stitch the seam and strip together. Trim the seam allowances, then finish the seam-covering strip as you did before.

5. Repeat the same process until all of the diagonal rows are stitched together.

# BINDING

Bind the edges of your quilt with straight-grain strips of the dark print or follow Judy's suggestion below.

## *Judy's Binding Suggestion*

Judy added a wider-than-usual binding, which required adding an extra strip of batting all around.

1. Measure all 4 edges of your quilt. Cut 1½"-wide strips from batting to match the measurements. The batting strip is cut twice the desired finished width of the finished binding.
2. Using a wide zigzag stitch, join the batting strip to the edge of the quilt.

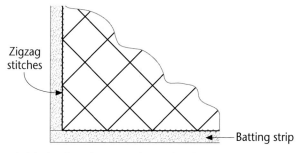

Zigzag stitches

Batting strip

3. Add the binding to the sides first, then to the top and bottom edges. See "Binding with Measured Strips" on page 91.

# Twelve Hours of Sunshine

*Twelve Hours of Sunshine by Jan Mullen, 1994, Perth, Western Australia, 60" x 75". Finished block size: 13" x 13".*

THE PINNACLES, 172 MILES NORTH OF PERTH IN NAMBUNG NATIONAL PARK. PHOTO BY PHOTO INDEX.

*P*erth is known for its clear, sunny skies and many long, hot days in summer, so here's our little bit of sunshine for you.

One of my clever staff, Jan Mullen, loves all things celestial, especially stars. In fact, she has taught a number of star quilt classes. With her art-teacher training, Jan likes to experiment with shapes and colours and enjoys the creative challenge of designing her own original quilts.

For the quilt she chose the sun as her theme and constructed the twelve suns and their borders in a slightly abstract manner that is easy to piece.

As every quilter knows, the fabric search sometimes involves compromise. We really wanted a cream and gold background, but that particular fabric was no longer available. Heard that before?

PERTH IS BILLED AS THE "SUNSHINE CITY" BECAUSE IT AVERAGES EIGHT HOURS OF SUNSHINE DAILY THROUGHOUT THE YEAR.

## MATERIALS: *44"-wide fabric*

½ yd. each of 12 gold prints for suns, sashings, inner border, and binding
1¾ yds. light print for background
¼ yd. gold print for middle border
⅜ yd. each of 5 cream prints for outer border
4½ yds. for backing
64" x 80" piece of batting
Paper suitable for sewing on (lightweight brown paper, typing, or copier paper)

# Sewing on Paper

- Use ¼"-wide seam allowances.
- Set the stitch length on your machine for a short stitch (approximately 18 to 20 stitches per inch). This makes it easier to remove the paper later.
- Starting in the centre of the paper, pin 2 fabric strips right sides together onto the paper. Sew the 2 strips together, through the paper, back-stitching at the beginning and end of each seam. With an iron set on the *cotton* setting, carefully press the seam open.
- Trim away excess fabric, leaving a ¼"-wide seam allowance for appliqué pieces; trim even with the paper for sashings and borders.

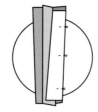

For appliqué pieces

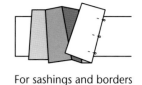

For sashings and borders

- Add a new strip to each of the first 2 strips. Sew, press, and trim. Continue until the paper is covered. Always leave an overhang but backstitch on the paper.

## Using the Free-Form Method to Cut Uneven Strips

Stack 4 to 6 fabrics at a time and use a rotary cutter and ruler to cut fabric into uneven strips. For instance, if the directions call for approximately 1"-wide strips, cut the strips by tapering them from 1½" on one side to 1" on the other and from ¾" to 1" as shown. Follow the same guidelines for making uneven 3" and uneven 4" strips.

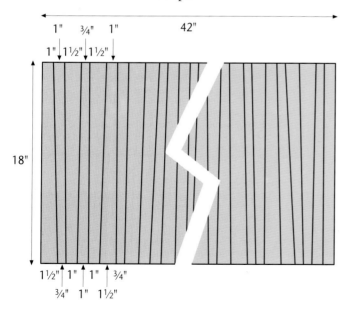

## Sun Centres

1. Draw twelve 7" to 8" circles onto paper and cut them out.
2. Using the free-form cutting method, cut 6 uneven 1" strips from the lengthwise grain of each of the 12 gold fabrics. Cut each strip in half so that you have 12 strips, each 9" long. You will use 1 strip of each fabric in each block.
3. Working from the centre to the outer edges, sew the strips to the circles, using the sewing-on-paper method. Trim away the excess fabric, leaving ¼" outside the paper circle. Each sun centre will have 10 to 12 different gold fabric strips.

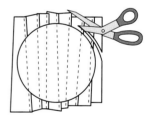

Trim to ¼" around outside of circle.

4. Press the ¼"-wide seam allowance over the paper circle. Carefully remove the paper, working from one side of the circle to the other. Press the seam allowance on the outside edge of the circle again if necessary.

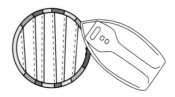

# SUN RAYS

1. Cut 1 strip, 4" x 18", from each of the 12 gold fabrics. Cut 1 additional 4" x 18" strip from 3 of the gold fabrics.
2. Stack the strips. From each of the strips, cut pieces that measure approximately 3" on one side and ¼" on the other as shown. Centre the ¼"-wide end with the 3"-wide end. You should be able to cut 10 sun rays from each 18"-long strip. Cut 144 sun rays.

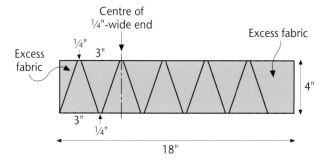

3. Press under ¼"-wide seam allowances on the long sides of the sun rays. You will trim the points when you appliqué the rays in place.

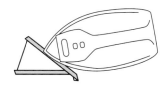

## BACKGROUND BLOCKS

1. From the background fabric, cut 12 squares, each 13¾" x 13¾".
2. Pin a sun centre in the middle of each background square. Use only 1 pin.
3. Arrange the sun's rays in each block, tucking the raw edges under the sun centre. Adjust the rays as necessary so that there are few gaps or overlaps where the rays meet the edges of the sun centres. Pin the rays in place.
4. Appliqué all the pieces to the background squares, using the traditional appliqué stitch. (See page 84.) To make sharp points on the sun rays, refer to "Helpful Hints" on page 85.

## ASSEMBLING THE QUILT TOP

### Sashings and Inner Border

1. Make paper foundations for the sashing and inner border strips. Tape or glue pieces of paper together if necessary to achieve the length required. Make the following paper strips:

8 Strip A, each 3" x 14", for sashing strips
3 Strip B, each 3" x 46", for sashing strips
2 Strip C, each 3" x 64", for inner border strips
2 Strip D, each 3" x 52", for inner border strips

2. From the 12 gold fabrics, cut 4" x 18" strips. You will need approximately 32 to 36 strips. Using the free-form cutting method, cut uneven 4" strips from the 18"-long strips as shown.

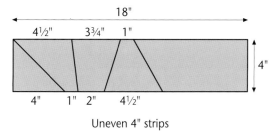

Uneven 4" strips

3. Working from the centre of each paper foundation, sew the fabric strips in place. Trim fabric even with paper. Carefully remove the paper.
4. Trim and square up each block to 13½" x 13½". (See page 86.) Sew the blocks and sashing strips A together into 4 horizontal rows. Press the seams towards the sashing strips. Join the rows together, sewing sashing strips B in place. Press the seam allowances towards the sashing strips.

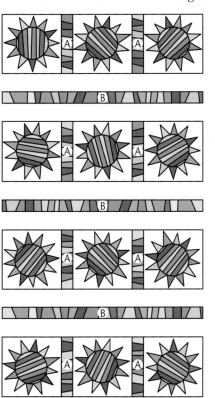

5. Sew inner border strips C to the sides, then sew inner border strips D to the top and bottom edges. Press seams as you did earlier.

## Middle Border

1. From the crosswise grain of the middle border fabric, cut 7 strips, each 1" wide. Join them together, end to end.
2. Sew the middle border in place, following the directions on pages 86–87 for straight-cut borders. Press seam allowances towards the border.

## Outer Border

1. Make paper foundations for the outer border strips.

   2 side borders, each 5" x 68"
   2 top and bottom borders, each 5" x 62"

2. From the 5 cream fabrics, cut 5" x 42" strips. You will need approximately 8 to 12 strips. Using the free-form cutting method, cut uneven 3" to 4" strips from the 42"-long strips.
3. Sew the fabric strips to the paper foundations as you did before. Trim fabric even with paper. Carefully remove the paper.
4. Sew the outer border in place as you did with the middle border.

## FINISHING THE QUILT

1. Layer the quilt top with batting and backing; baste.
2. Quilt as desired.
3. Bind the edges with 2½"-wide strips cut from varying lengths of the gold fabrics. Join the strips, end to end. See "Attaching the Binding" on page 91.

A FLIGHT FROM SYDNEY TO PERTH TAKES
4 HOURS AND 20 MINUTES; THE RAIL TRIP ACROSS
THE CONTINENT ON THE "INDIAN PACIFIC"
TAKES THREE DAYS.

# Susan's Sunflowers

*Susan's Sunflowers by Susan Readhead, 1994, Perth, Western Australia, 23" x 30".*

*"Sunflowers often grow to a magnificent size. At a meeting of the Horticultural Society in August, 1832, a sunflower was exhibited whose disk measured four feet and six inches in circumference. It is said that in Peru and Mexico, its native country, the Helianthus annus often grows 20 feet in height and bears flowers 2 feet in diameter"* (Herman Bourne, The Florist's Manual, Boston, 1833).

Most people seem to love sunflowers because they are such a "happy" flower. Susan was inspired to make the wall hanging after taking a decorative wall-quilt class with Judy Turner last year. With the marvellous range of floral fabrics now available, you could design your own bouquet and fuse it to a background made with squares.

THE OLGAS IN THE DISTANCE, NORTHERN TERRITORY. PHOTO BY BETTY METZ.

## MATERIALS: *44"-wide fabric*

1 yd. (total) of 7 different sunflower prints for background and binding*
¼ yd. yellow solid for inner border
¾ yd. medium green small-scale check for outer border and bow
¼ yd. green solid for stems
¼ yd. large-scale sunflower print for appliqués
1 yd. fabric for backing
1 yd. craft batting (polyester fleece or a bonded or needle-punched batting)
¼ yd. paper-backed fusible web, such as HeatnBond® or Wonder-Under®

*This yardage allows for a pieced binding, using varying lengths of the sunflower fabrics. If you want a single-fabric binding, you will need ⅓ yard of fabric.*

## CUTTING

Cut all strips from the crosswise grain of the fabrics.

*From each of 7 sunflower prints, cut:*
1 strip, 3" x 42"; crosscut into 10 squares, each 3" x 3", to yield 70 squares
3"-wide strips of varying lengths to equal the measurement of the outside edges of your quilt. For a single fabric binding, cut 4 strips, each 3" x 42".

*From the yellow solid fabric, cut:*
4 strips, each 1¼" x 42", for the inner border.

*From the small-scale green checked fabric, cut:*
4 strips, each 3" x 42", for outer border
1 strip, 5" x 42", for bow

*From the green solid fabric, cut:*
3 strips, each 1" x 42", for the stems.

## ASSEMBLING THE QUILT TOP

*Use accurate ¼"-wide seam allowances.*

1. Arrange the squares of sunflower fabrics in an order that pleases you in 10 rows of 7 blocks each. Arrange them randomly or in a pattern.

## Helpful Hints

- *To avoid confusion when you sew the squares together, refer to "Chain Piecing & Matching Seams" on page 83 before sewing the squares together.*
- *Alternate the stitching direction from row to row to avoid "bowing" seams. Place a pin at the end of the stitching line so you will know at which end to begin stitching when adding the next row. Some quilters find it handy to keep even-numbered fabric strips on the top and odd-numbered strips on the bottom when sewing the strips together.*

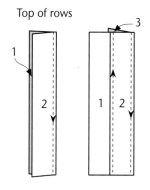

Top of rows

2. Sew the squares together into rows. Press the seams to one side, alternating the direction from row to row.
3. Join the rows, making sure to match the seams between the squares.
4. Add the inner border, then the outer border, measuring and cutting as directed for borders with straight-cut corners on pages 86–87.

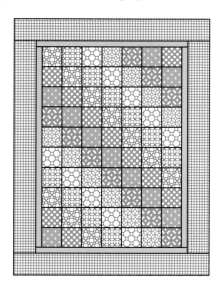

## APPLIQUÉ

1. Following the manufacturer's directions, apply the fusible web to the wrong side of your large-scale sunflower print.
2. Using a sharp pair of small scissors, cut out the flowers you would like to appliqué to the background. Study the size, colour, and shape of the flowers. Carefully cut around the outlines of the flowers, creating your own shapes where petals may be misshapen.
3. Peel away the paper backing and pin the flowers in place on the background. Arrange the flowers, adding layers to make a bouquet. Decide which 3 flowers should have stems. When you like the arrangement, fuse all of the flowers in place, except for the 3 flowers that will have stems, following the manufacturer's directions. Allow to cool.
4. To make the stems, fold each of the 1"-wide stem strips in half lengthwise, wrong sides together, and press with a steam iron. Arrange the stems on the background, tucking the top end of the stems under the flower appliqué. Pin in place. Using small running stitches, sew the strips to the background, about ¼" from the raw edge. Roll the folded edge over the seam allowance. Appliqué the folded edge to the background. When you appliqué the bottom end of the stem, turn under a ⅛"- to ¼"-wide seam allowance. Fuse the remaining 3 flower appliqués in place.

## FINISHING THE QUILT

1. Layer quilt top with batting and backing; baste.
2. Quilt as desired. Susan machine quilted the background squares in a cross-hatched grid (as shown on page 88) and hand quilted a double cable in the outer border. Crosshatch the entire quilt top if you desire.
3. Bind the edges with the strips of a sunflower print. (See pages 90–91.)
4. Add the bow. Fold the 5"-wide green checked strip in half lengthwise, right sides together. Sew the 2 long sides together and 1 short side together to form a tube. Turn the tube right side out. Press, then topstitch the open end closed. Tie a bow and pin in place. Stitch the bow to the quilt.

# Australian Country Cottages

*Australian country cottages by Margaret Rolfe, 1994, Canberra, ACT, Australia, 84" x 56".*

*The late afternoon sun shines its glorious golden light through the gum trees on this old Australian homestead.*

For more than 20 years, I have been collecting houses—house ornaments, that is—from all over the world. Made from different materials, such as wood, clay, and china, they remind me of places visited, friends' gifts, and life's memories.

So far, I have lived in sixteen houses. Two of my favourites were a little pink weatherboard and a limestone workman's cottage that my daughter and I lived in during the early days of The Calico House. After renovating them both, I was reluctant to let them go. But that's the thing with houses—you often have to move on and remember the happy times spent under that roof!

Margaret is a well-known and respected quilter and author. She, too, loves Australian houses. She and Beryl Hodges wrote **Australian Houses in Patchwork**. Margaret also wrote **Go Wild with Quilts** (That Patchwork Place).

## MATERIALS: *44"-wide fabric*

2¼ yds. light prints for background, cornerstones, and inner border
1¾ yds. assorted dark plaids for roofs and pieced outer border
1 yd. assorted light plaids for walls and chimneys
¼ yd. assorted dark prints for windows and doors
1¾ yds. dark plaid for sashing strips and binding
4¼ yds. for backing
88" x 60" piece of batting

THE POPULATION OF AUSTRALIA IS 17 MILLION PEOPLE. ITS SHEEP POPULATION IS 170 MILLION.

# MAKING THE COTTAGE BLOCKS

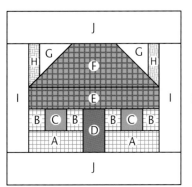

Cottage Block
Finished size: 12" x 12"
Make 15.

1. Cut the background pieces (G, I, and J) for *all 15* Cottage blocks.

*From the* lengthwise *grain of the background fabric, cut:*
1 strip, 3⅛" wide; crosscut into 15 squares, each 3⅛" x 3⅛"; cut squares once diagonally to yield 30 half-square triangles for G
4 strips, each 2" wide; crosscut into 30 pieces, each 2" x 8", for I
6 strips, each 2¾" wide; crosscut into 30 pieces, each 2¾" x 12½", for J

2. Refer to the cutting guide below and cut out the remaining pieces to complete 15 Cottage blocks. As you cut out the pieces for each cottage, lay the pieces out in their correct places on a large square of paper. By doing this, you can stack the cottages on top of each other and take the stack to your sewing machine.

## Cutting Guide for 1 Cottage Block
*All pieces include ¼"-wide seam allowances.*

| Piece | # to Cut | Fabric | Size |
|-------|----------|--------|------|
| A | 2 | light plaid | 2" x 4¼" |
| B | 4 | light plaid | 2" x 1⅝" |
| C | 2 | dark print | 2" x 2" |
| D | 1 | dark print | 2" x 3½" |
| E | 1 | dark plaid | 2" x 9½" |
| F | 1 | dark plaid | 3½" x 10¼"* |
| H | 2 | light plaid | 1¼" x 3⅞"** |

*Trim both ends at a 45° angle as shown to make roof shape.

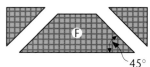

**Trim 1 end of 1 piece at a 45° angle; trim 1 end of the other piece in the opposite direction as shown.

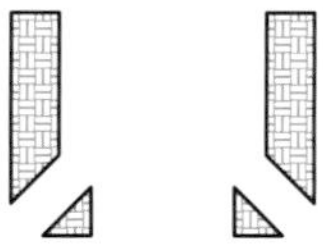

# ASSEMBLING THE BLOCKS

*Use accurate ¼"-wide seam allowances.*

1. Piece 15 cottages as shown.

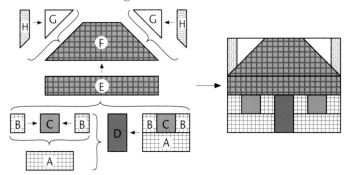

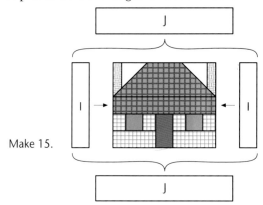

2. Stitch Piece I to the side edges, and Piece J to the top and bottom edges of each block.

Make 15.

3. Press each block. Measure each block and trim as necessary so that they are exactly 12½" square.

# ASSEMBLING THE QUILT TOP

*From the lengthwise grain of the background fabric, cut:*
2 strips, each 2½" x 72½", for side inner border
2 strips, each 2½" x 48½", for top and bottom inner border
1 strip, 2½" x 61"; crosscut into 24 squares, each 2½" x 2½", for cornerstones

*From the crosswise grain of the sashing fabric, cut:*
13 strips, each 2½" x 42"; crosscut into 38 pieces, each 2½" x 12½", for sashing strips.

1. Stitch the cornerstones and sashing strips together into 6 horizontal rows. Press the seam allowances towards the sashing strips.

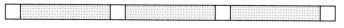

Make 6.

2. Stitch sashing strips to the Cottage blocks, making 5 horizontal rows of 3 cottages each.

Make 5.

3. Join the rows of cottages and sashing strips together.

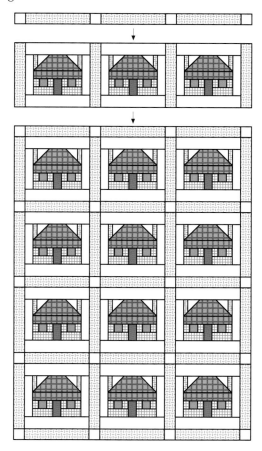

4. Sew the left and right inner border strips to the sides of the quilt top. Then join the top and bottom inner borders to the quilt top.

5. From the remaining pieces of dark plaid fabrics, cut 66 squares, each 4½" x 4½", for the outer border. Stitch 19 squares together for each of the side borders. Stitch 14 squares together for each of the top and bottom borders. Sew the outer borders to the sides, then to the top and bottom edges of the quilt top.

Top and Bottom Outer Borders
Make 2.

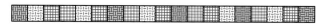

Side Outer Borders
Make 2.

## FINISHING THE QUILT

1. Layer quilt top with batting and backing; baste.
2. Quilt as desired. Margaret outline-quilted around each piece, ¼" away from the seams. See "Marking the Quilting Design" on page 88.
3. Bind with 3"-wide straight-grain strips of dark plaid fabric. (See pages 90–91.)

AUSTRALIA IS ABOUT THE SIZE
OF THE CONTIGUOUS UNITED STATES.

# Under the Southern Cross

*Under the Southern Cross by Wendy Sier, 1994, Perth, Western Australia, 60" x 84".*

*Skyline of Perth at dusk. Later, the Southern Cross will be visible in the night sky.*

There is a line in our national anthem, "Advance Australia Fair," that states, "Beneath our radiant Southern Cross, we'll toil with hearts and hands . . ."*

One of the shop's first patchwork teachers, Wendy Sier, drew inspiration for this quilt from that verse. As someone who came to live in Australia from England, Wendy loves our brilliant day and night skies and the relaxed lifestyle that we lead here in "the West." A keen gardener and bush walker, Wendy still finds time to make quilts.

The star-filled quilt on page 32 combines two traditional blocks, Indian Star and Judy's Star, with a Sawtooth border. It reminds Wendy of the constellation, visible in the southern night sky, that guided the first settlers across the oceans from Europe to Australia.

The Southern Cross is on our flag and in our national anthem and has a special place in our hearts.

*Composed by 'Amicus' (Peter Dodds McCormick 1835–1916)

PERTH'S SISTER CITIES ARE HOUSTON AND SAN DIEGO IN THE UNITED STATES, KAGOSHIMA IN JAPAN, AND RHODES AND MEGISTI IN GREECE.

## MATERIALS: *44"-wide fabric*

⅓ yd. each of 8 different dark blue prints for block backgrounds
⅓ yd. each of 8 different gold prints for blocks and Sawtooth middle border
⅝ yd. gold solid for inner border
½ yd. dark blue print for Sawtooth middle border
2 yds. blue-and-gold print for outer border
¾ yd. blue solid for binding
5 yds. for backing
64" x 80" piece of batting

# Making the Blocks

*Use accurate ¼"-wide seam allowances.*

## Indian Star

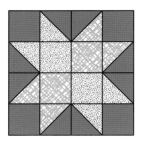

Indian Star
Finished size: 12" x 12"
Make 8.

For each block, choose 1 dark blue and 2 gold print fabrics. Make 8 blocks. The cutting directions below are for 1 block.

*From a dark blue print fabric, cut:*
4 squares, each 3½" x 3½", for A
4 squares, each 3⅞" x 3⅞"; crosscut once diagonally to yield 8 triangles for B

*From each of 2 gold print fabrics, cut:*
2 squares, each 3½" x 3½", for C
2 squares, each 3⅞" x 3⅞"; crosscut once diagonally to yield 4 triangles for D

Piece 8 blocks as shown. Press seams towards the dark blue print.

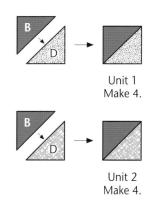

Unit 1
Make 4.

Unit 2
Make 4.

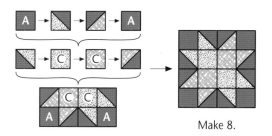

Make 8.

## Judy's Star

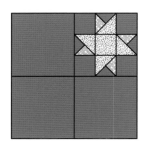

Judy's Star
Finished size: 12" x 12"
Make 7.

For each block, choose 1 dark blue and 2 gold print fabrics. Make 7 blocks; each block should have a different combination of 3 fabrics. The cutting directions below are for 1 block.

*From a dark blue print fabric, cut:*
3 squares, each 6½" x 6½", for A
4 squares, each 2½" x 2½", for B
1 square, 3¼" x 3¼"; crosscut twice diagonally to yield 4 triangles for C

*From first gold print fabric, cut:*
1 square, 2½" x 2½", for D
2 squares, each 2⅞" x 2⅞"; crosscut once diagonally to yield 4 triangles for E

*From second gold print fabric, cut:*
1 square, 3¼" x 3¼"; crosscut twice diagonally to yield 4 triangles for F

1. Piece the star patch first as shown. The finished size is 6".

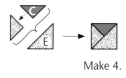

Make 4.

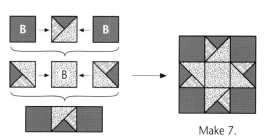

Make 7.

2. Complete the block by adding the 6½" x 6½" blue squares (piece A) as shown.

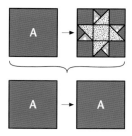

## ASSEMBLING THE QUILT TOP

1. Arrange the completed blocks, referring to the colour photo on page 32.
2. Sew the blocks together in 5 rows of 3 blocks each.
3. Add the inner border, measuring and cutting as directed for straight-cut borders on pages 86–87. Cut 3½"-wide strips from the crosswise grain of the gold solid fabric. Piece the strips together, end to end, as necessary.
4. Make the Sawtooth middle border.

*From dark blue middle border print fabric, cut:*
36 squares, each 3⅞" x 3⅞"; crosscut once diagonally to yield 72 triangles
4 squares, each 3½" x 3½"

*From gold print fabrics, cut:*
36 squares, each 3⅞" x 3⅞"; crosscut once diagonally to yield 72 triangles

Make 72 squares from the dark blue and gold triangles. Press seam allowances towards the dark fabric.

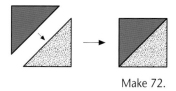

Make 72.

For each side middle border, stitch 22 pieced squares together.

For the top and bottom middle borders, stitch 14 pieced squares together; add 3½" x 3½" dark blue squares to each end of the 2 border strips.

Top and Bottom Middle Borders
Make 2.

Side Middle Borders
Make 2.

Sew the side middle borders in place, then add the top and bottom borders.

5. Measure the quilt top again, including the inner and middle borders. Cut 6½"-wide strips from the crosswise grain of the outer border fabric. Piece the strips together, end to end, as necessary. Sew the outer borders in place.

## FINISHING THE QUILT

1. Layer the quilt top with batting and backing; baste.
2. Quilt as desired or follow the quilting suggestion.
3. Bind the edges with 2½"-wide strips cut from the blue solid fabric. (See pages 90–91.)

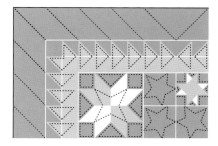

Quilting Suggestion

# Down on the Farm

*Down on the Farm by Kathy Oliver, 1994, Gnowangerup, Western Australia, 26" x 38½".*

At the Calico House, we really value our country customers and realize the important role that crafts of all kinds play in their lives. Each day, parcels, large and small, are sent out to the far-flung corners of our vast state and country.

When I first married, we lived on a remote 4,000-acre property in the south of Western Australia. As I was 450 miles from my home city, I tried every conceivable craft, participated in correspondence courses, grew all our vegetables, and helped in the cattle yards. After Sarah arrived, I even started a kindergarten. More important, I grew to appreciate the down-to-earth qualities of country folk. I have always admired their sincerity, honesty, and sense of humour, even in adversity.

The maker of the quilt, Kathy Oliver, a primary school teacher, writes, "I have been really excited by the American patchwork designs which depict specific rural environments. When I designed this quilt, I was living in the Great Southern Region of Western Australia. I saw so many possibilities for patchwork

A typical scene on a working Australian farm: the woolly sheep being penned for shearing, a farmer in a well-worn hat, and the ever-present brown dog.

from everything that surrounded me." Kathy modeled the farmer on those she saw around her—with their short trousers, often called "stubbies," and hairy chests peeking out over the top of navy blue singlets, ideal for the hot summer weather. Chickens are called "chooks," and most rural properties are incomplete without the "chook pen" in the backyard. The Kangaroo Paw is a native flower of Australia and our State Flower. The mountain range represents the Stirling Ranges, a unique feature of the Great Southern Region.

## BEFORE YOU BEGIN

Although this quilt has a lot of pieces, you will find it easy to make if you read all instructions before beginning. Refer to the photograph of the quilt for colour-placement ideas.

## MATERIALS: 44"-wide fabric
*Refer to quilt photo and the instructions for fabric information.*

24 fat eighths (9" x 22") of assorted fabrics for blocks which should include the following:
- dark blue plaid for mountains
- medium blue plaid for mountains
- light blue for sky
- black solid for black sheep and tractor wheels
- black print for black sheep
- green for Kangaroo Paw background
- green for kangaroo paw
- light green print for kangaroo paw

⅛ yd. yellow check for Wheat and Mountains foreground and Cow background

⅛ yd. yellow-and-white plaid for Wheat and Mountains background

¼ yd. golden yellow for wheat appliqués

½ yd. muslin for Black Sheep, Farmer and His Dog, Chickens, and Tractor backgrounds

½ yd. burgundy solid for framing strips, outer border, and 1 piece each in the Kangaroo Paw and Farmer and His Dog blocks

1 yd. dark green print for sashing and inner border

¼ yd. for binding

⅔ yd. for backing

30" x 42" piece of low-loft batting

Assorted colors of embroidery thread

2 buttons for the centre of the tractor wheels

*Kathy used prints, plaids, checks, and solid fabrics.*

# MAKING THE BLOCKS

It is essential to use accurate ¼"-wide seam allowances. Be sure seam allowances are marked and cut precisely so the pieces will fit together accurately.

The background for appliqué blocks is cut 1½" larger than the finished size to compensate for the fabric "drawing up" during appliqué. It is better to cut the blocks a little larger, then trim them after the appliqué is complete.

When templates or patterns are provided for the blocks, make sturdy templates for the pieces. Refer to "Making Templates" on page 84. Use the patterns on the pullout pattern insert.

Appliqué the pieces in the order indicated on the patterns. See "Appliqué Techniques" on pages 84–86.

All bias strips for appliqué are cut ⅝" wide unless otherwise noted. Refer to "Appliqué Stems or Animal Legs" on page 86.

Embroidery stitches are on page 89.

## *Helpful Hints*

*Fold the bias strips into thirds lengthwise, making sure the raw edges will not show on the front side. Finger-press. Tack the raw edges together with a running stitch.*

## Wheat and Mountains Block

Finished size (without frame): 22½" x 6½"

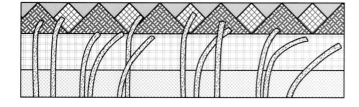

*From the yellow checked fabric, cut:*
1 strip, 2½" x 23", for the wheat-field foreground

*From the yellow-and-white plaid fabric, cut:*
1 strip, 3" x 23", for the wheat-field background

*From the dark blue plaid fabric, cut:*
2 squares, each 5½" x 5½", for mountains. Crosscut each square twice diagonally to yield 8 triangles. You will use 6 triangles for the block.

*From the medium blue plaid fabric, cut:*
1 strip, 2" x 14"; crosscut into 7 squares, each 2" x 2". You will use 6 squares for the mountains.

*From the light blue fabric, cut:*
3 squares, each 3⅜" x 3⅜"; crosscut each square twice diagonally to yield 12 triangles. You will use 11 triangles for the sky.

1. Sew the 2 wheat-field foreground and background strips together along the long sides.
2. Sew the light blue triangles to the medium blue squares. Make 5 units that contain 2 triangles; make a left side unit as shown.

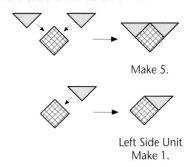

Make 5.

Left Side Unit
Make 1.

3. Sew the units that you just completed to the dark blue triangles to form the mountain range.

4. Centre mountain strip on the wheat background strip and sew them together. You will trim the ends later when you square up the block.

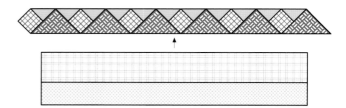

5. Make bias strips for the wheat appliqués. From the wheat appliqué fabric, cut 12 bias strips, each ⅝" x 6". Prepare the strips as directed on page 86. Arrange the wheat stalks on the background, referring to the colour photo on page 36 for placement. Appliqué in place, turning under the ends of each wheat stalk.
6. Embroider wheat heads, using straight stitches and 2 or 3 shades of gold or yellow embroidery thread.

## Cow Block

Finished size (without frame): 8¼" x 6½"

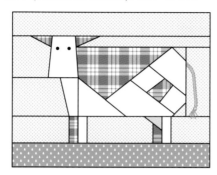

*From the yellow checked fabric, cut:*
Pieces 2, 4, 7, 15, 16, 17, 18, 21, 25, and 27

*From the muslin, cut:*
Pieces 5, 6, 8, 10, 11, 12, 14, 20, and 24

*From the assorted fabrics, cut:*
Pieces 1, 3, 9, 13, 19, 22, 23, and 26. Be sure the fabric for piece 26 is darker than the background pieces.

1. Join the pieces in units as shown.

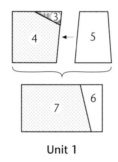

Unit 1

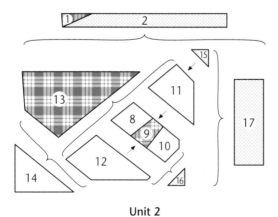

Unit 2

Unit 3

2. Sew the units together to complete the block.

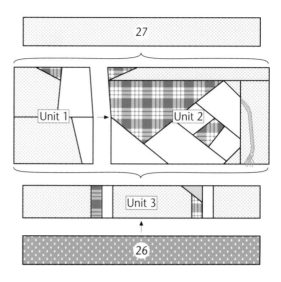

3. Kathy embroidered a line of outline stitches to help define the cow's head (between Piece 5 and Pieces 6 and 7). Embroider the cow's eyes, using French knots. Embroider a bell, using satin stitches. For the cow's tail, cut three 3"-long pieces of embroidery floss and knot one end of each. From the back of the block, bring each length of floss to the front, in the seam that joins Pieces 11, 15, and 17. Braid the 3 lengths together and knot the end, leaving a little bit of a tassel at the tip of the tail.

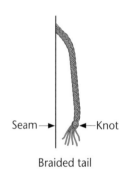

Braided tail

## Kangaroo Paw and Black Sheep Block

Finished size (without frame): 10¾" x 5¾"

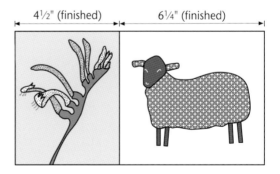

1. From the muslin, cut 1 rectangle, 6¾" x 6¼", for the black sheep background.
2. From the green fabric, cut 1 rectangle 5" x 6¼",

for the kangaroo paw background.

3. Make templates for all of the appliqué pieces.
4. Cut out the appliqué pieces.

*From the green fabric for kangaroo paw, cut:*
Pieces 1–9 (petals)

*From the burgundy fabric, cut:*
Piece 10 (stem)

*From the light green print fabric, cut:*
Pieces 11–12 (flowers)

*From the black print fabric, cut:*
Pieces 5–7 (Sheep A)

*From the black solid fabric, cut:*
Piece 8 (Sheep A)

5. Make bias strip for the sheep's legs. From the black solid fabric, cut 1 bias strip, ⅝" x 7". Prepare the strip as directed on page 86.
6. Appliqué the sheep and the kangaroo paw pieces onto their background blocks, in the order indicated on the patterns. Refer to the colour photo on page 36 for placement of the pieces within the block. Kathy used fusible web to fuse the kangaroo paw stem and flowers in place, first. Then she machine stitched around the outside edges of each fused piece, using a small satin stitch.
7. Embroider the sheep's eyes and nose, using outline stitches. Using straight stitches or small satin stitches, embroider buds at the tips of the petals. At the ends of the flowers, embroider the details with straight stitches and French knots.
8. Sew the blocks together along the 6¼"-long sides, referring to the block plan on page 39. Press the seam towards the Kangaroo Paw block.
9. Square up the block and trim it to 11¼" x 6¼". Refer to "Squaring Up the Blocks" on page 86.

## Farmer and His Dog Block
Finished size (without frame): 8¼" x 11"

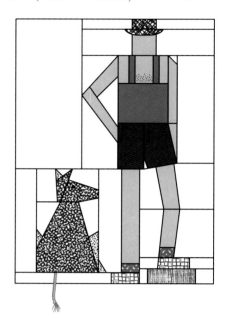

*From the muslin, cut:*
1 each of Pieces 1, 3, 4, 6, 8, 10, 11, 18, 24, 25, 27, 30, 31, 32, 34, 35, 37, 39, 43, 45, 46, 49, 51, 53, 54, and 56

*From the assorted scraps, cut:*
all of the remaining pieces, except Piece 36

*From the burgundy solid fabric, cut:*
1 Piece 36

1. Join the pieces in units as shown.

**NOTE:** Before sewing Rows A and B together, make the hat brim (Piece 57) as directed in step 3, page 41. Layer Row A, the hat brim, and Row B, right sides together. Place the centre of the brim in the centre of Pieces 2 and 5, aligning the raw edges of the seam allowances. Sew them together.

---

### Tea Dyeing

Boil 2 to 4 tea bags in 1 gallon of water for approximately 20 minutes. (This will depend on the depth of colour you desire.) Remove the tea bags and add the fabric. Simmer for 10 to 30 minutes (again depending on the depth of colour desired). Stir occasionally.

Remove the fabric and rinse thoroughly. (I use cold water and find that very little of the colour comes out.) Next, place the fabric in a solution of white vinegar and water (approximately half a cup to 1 gallon of water). Rinse thoroughly and hang to dry; when still slightly damp, press.

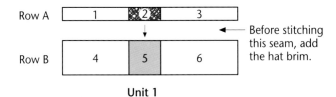

Row A | 1 | 2 | 3

→ Before stitching this seam, add the hat brim.

Row B | 4 | 5 | 6

**Unit 1**

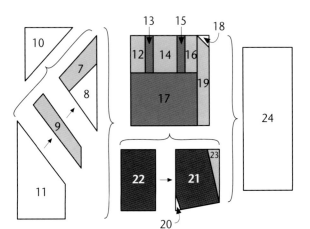

10
7
8
9
11

13  15  18
12  14  16
19
17

23
**22** → **21**
20

24

**Unit 2**

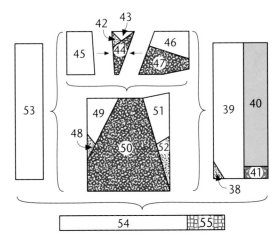

42  43
45 → 44
46
47

53

49  51
48
**50**  52

39  40
38
41

54  55

**Unit 3**

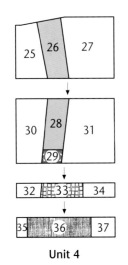

25  26  27

30  28  31
29

32  33  34

35  36  37

**Unit 4**

2. Sew the units together to complete the block.

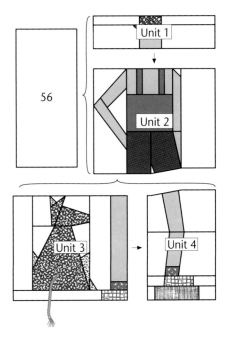

56

Unit 1

Unit 2

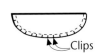

Unit 3  →  Unit 4

3. With right sides to-gether, stitch the 2 blue Piece 57 together along the curved edge, using a ¼"-wide seam allowance. Trim the seam to ⅛" wide and clip it to create a smooth curve. Turn right sides out.

Trim seam allowance to ⅛".

Clips

4. Embroider details on the completed block. Kathy used stem stitches to embroider the crows in flight, straight stitches in a random pattern for the hair on the farmer's chest, and running stitches for the details on the farmer's shorts. Use satin stitches for the dog's nose and collar. For the dog's eye, make a French knot.

Make a braided tail for the dog. Refer to the direc-tions in step 3 of the Cow block on page 39.

Crows in Flight

## Sheep in the Paddock Block
Finished size (without frame): 10¾" x 7½"

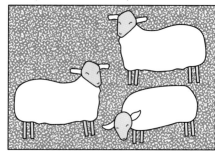

1. From the dark green print fabric, cut 1 rectangle, 9½" x 12¼", for the background.
2. Make templates for all of the appliqué pieces. You will make 1 Sheep A, 1 Sheep A reversed, and 1 Sheep B.
3. From assorted scraps, cut the appliqué pieces.
4. Make bias strips for the sheep's legs. From fabric for sheep's legs, cut 3 strips, each ⅝" x 7". Prepare the strips as directed on page 86.
5. Appliqué the sheep in the order indicated on the patterns. Refer to the colour photo on page 36 for placement of the pieces within the block.
6. Embroider the sheep eyes and noses, using outline stitches.

## Chickens Block
Finished size (without frame): 9¾" x 4"

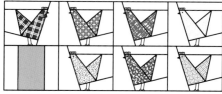

Completed Chickens Block

Individual Chicken Block

### Hen Blocks
*Directions are for making 1 block.*

1. From the muslin, cut 1 each of Pieces 1, 4, 5, 6, and 7. From the assorted fat eighths, cut 1 each of Pieces 2 and 3.
2. Join the pieces as shown to make Unit 1. Make 6.

### Rooster Block
*The Rooster block is the same as the Hen block, only in reverse.*

1. From the muslin, cut 1 each of Pieces 1, 4, 5, 6, and 7 *reversed*. From the assorted fat eighths, cut 1 each of Pieces 2 and 3 *reversed*.
2. Join the pieces as shown to make Unit 2. Make 1.

## Post Block

1. From the muslin, cut 1 each of Pieces 8 and 10. From the assorted fat eighths, cut 1 Piece 9.
2. Join the pieces as shown to make Unit 3. Make 1.

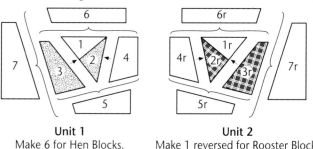

**Unit 1**
Make 6 for Hen Blocks.

**Unit 2**
Make 1 reversed for Rooster Block.

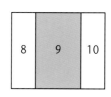

**Unit 3**
Make 1 for Post Block.

# Assembling the Chickens Block

1. Sew the units together to complete the Chickens block, referring to the block plan to the right and to the photo on page 36.

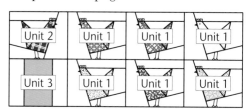

2. Embroider the details on the completed block. Use French knots for the chickens' eyes, and straight stitches for their beaks, legs, and combs. Embroider the rooster's wattle with straight stitches.

## Tractor Block
Finished size (without frame): 10¾" x 7½"

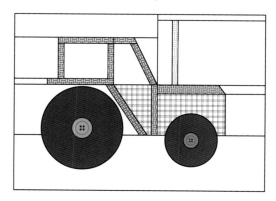

*From the muslin, cut:*
1 each of Pieces 1, 3, 4, 6, 8, 9, 12, 14, 17, 18, 20, 24, and 25

*From 1 fat eighth, cut:*
1 each of Pieces 7 and 22

*From another fat eighth, cut:*
1 each of Pieces 2, 5, 10, 11, 13, 15, 16, 19, 21, and 23

*From the black solid fabric, cut:*
1 each of the front and rear tractor wheels

1. Join the pieces in units as shown.

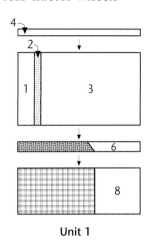

**Unit 1**

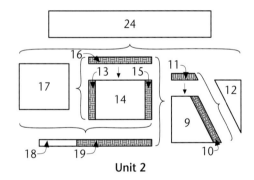

**Unit 2**

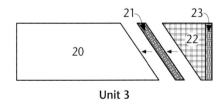

**Unit 3**

2. Sew Units 1, 2, 3, and Piece 25 together to complete the block.

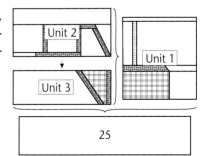

3. Make templates for the 2 wheels from stiff paper, such as a file folder. Do not add seam allowances to templates. Complete the circles, following the directions for "Appliqué Circles" on page 86.
4. Steam-press the circles, then let them cool for a couple of minutes. Carefully pull back the fabric and remove the paper circles. Gently pull the basting threads to tighten the seam allowance and make the circles lie flat.
5. Pin the circles in place on the tractor and appliqué with tiny stitches. Refer to the colour photo on page 36 for placement.
6. Sew a button in the centre of each tractor wheel.

## ADDING THE FRAMING STRIPS

*Each block, except the Wheat and Mountains block, is framed with a 1"-wide (cut) burgundy strip. The frames finish to ½" wide.*

*From the burgundy solid fabric, cut:*
10 strips, each 1" x 42". This will be enough for the outer border also.

Square up each block if necessary. (See page 86.) Measure the sides of each block, cut framing strips to match the measurement, and sew the strips to the right and left sides of each block. Press towards the frame. Measure the width of the block, including the frame, cut strips to match the measurement, and sew them to the top and bottom edges of the block. Press towards the frame.

## ASSEMBLING THE QUILT TOP

I encourage you to join the blocks in your own way. I arranged the blocks the way that appealed to me. The way that you arrange your blocks may depend a lot on the colour choices that you have made.

*From dark green fabric for sashing and inner border, cut:*
6 strips, each 2" x 42"
1 strip, 1¼" x 9¾"

1. Join the 1¼" x 9¾" sashing strip to the bottom edge of the Cow block as shown.

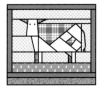

2. Join the Farmer and His Dog block to the bottom of the resulting unit. Add a 2"-wide sashing strip to the bottom edge of the Farmer and His Dog block. Sew a 2"-wide sashing strip to the right side of the resulting unit. Then add the Chickens block to the bottom edge to complete Unit 1.

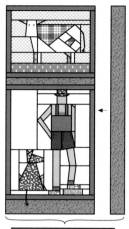

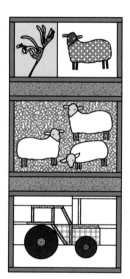

Unit 1

3. Join the Kangaroo Paw and Black Sheep, Sheep in the Paddock, and Tractor blocks with 2"-wide sashing strips as shown.

Unit 2

4. Square up and trim the Wheat and Mountains block to 7" x 23". Sew a 2"-wide sashing strip to the bottom edge to complete Unit 3.

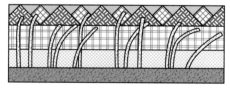

Unit 3

5. Sew Units 1, 2, and 3 together.

6. Add the green inner border strips, measuring and cutting as directed for straight-cut borders on pages 86–87.
7. Add the 1"-wide burgundy outer border strips that you cut at the same time as the framing strips, measuring and cutting as you did for the inner border.

## FINISHING THE QUILT

Prior to layering the quilt top with batting and backing, you may want to dye your patchwork to give it an aged look. Experiment with scraps to find the colour you like. Follow the tea dyeing "recipe" on page 40.

1. Layer the quilt top with batting and backing; baste.
2. Quilt as desired. Kathy machine quilted in-the-ditch around the each block design, using invisible nylon thread. The corners were then tied with stranded cotton, such as embroidery thread or perle cotton.
3. Bind the edges with 2½"-wide straight-grain strips of the binding fabric. (See pages 90–91.)

# Little Liberty

*Little Liberty by Wendy Sier, 1994, Perth, Western Australia, 26" x 36".*
*Hand quilted by Wendy, Jan Tocas, Jan Houghton, and Jenny Burke.*

*L*ike many others with a love of fine fabrics, I have always appreciated Liberty Tana™ Lawn. As a child, I eagerly awaited my much-loved Aunt Mona's return from her various trips. In the 1950s, very few Australians experienced the luxury of overseas travel.

Once, she presented me with a Japanese doll dressed in a fine silk kimono from Tokyo and green leather shoes from the Port of Aden. Another time it was special hair ribbons from Switzerland and books from England, which I shall cherish forever.

The best memory of all was when her six sisters (my mother included) were tossed a stylish silk scarf or a dress length of fabric from Liberty's. Even then, I admired their subtle designs and colours.

While working on Bond Street in London in 1969, I often wandered into the Liberty shop on nearby Regent Street. I marveled at the wooden staircase and balconies that were draped with exotic wares, such as Persian rugs and Indian quilts. Twenty-one years later, I found myself in their export department ordering Tana Lawn and country cotton for The Calico House.

Ever since opening my shop, I've stocked some Liberty fabrics—even if it is only for my own aesthetic pleasure. Liberty fabrics have such a timeless appeal and heirloom quality. The quilt on page 45 was made as a friendship quilt for a new baby.

## MATERIALS: *44"-wide fabric*

Assorted cotton prints that blend together and range from light to medium to dark values for blocks*
Assorted cotton prints in light, medium, and dark values for blocks*
1⅛ yds. solid for border and backing
¼ yd. print for binding
30" x 40" piece of batting
Paper for paper piecing

*Use prints that blend together and range from light to medium to dark values. You can use pieces that are left over from other projects or small swatches that you have collected. Wendy used Liberty fabrics exclusively, which are 36" wide. There are 213 diamonds in the quilt; each fabric is used only once.*

## BEFORE YOU BEGIN

Tumbling Blocks or Baby Blocks is a simple quilt design using only one shape: a diamond. It is ideal for a charm quilt or scrap quilt. To achieve the three-dimensional effect, make the desired number of cubes, using one dark, one medium, and one light value fabric in each cube and always orienting the cube the same way.

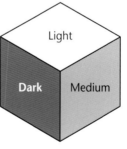

The method used is English or Paper Piecing. It ensures that the fabric shape remains stable while you stitch over a paper foundation. After you sew the diamonds together, you remove the paper.

Each cube has three values of one colour. The colours are grouped together; they blend and change across the quilt from dark to light.

# MAKING THE BLOCKS

1. Make sturdy templates for Templates A and B on page 84.
2. Using Template A, cut out 213 paper diamonds.
3. Place Template B on the wrong side of each of your fabrics. Be sure to align the shapes with the straight grain of the fabric. Trace around the template, then cut out the shape. Cut out 213 fabric diamonds.
4. Place a paper diamond in the centre of each fabric shape; pin. Fold the seam allowance over the paper and baste in place through the paper and both layers of fabric. Repeat until you have prepared all 213 fabric shapes.

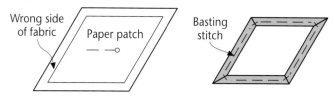

5. Arrange the prepared diamonds into groups of 3 values. Each group should have 1 light, 1 medium, and 1 dark diamond. Each group will form a cube, and you should have 71 cubes.
6. With right sides together, stitch 2 diamonds together along the folded edges of one side of the diamond. Use small stitches and try not to stitch through the paper. Be sure to line up the points. Backstitch at the beginning and end of each seam. Finger-press the seam open, then add the third diamond. Stitch them together on the remaining 2 sides of the diamond.

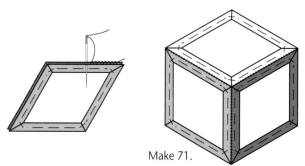

Make 71.

## ASSEMBLING THE QUILT TOP

1. Referring to the colour photo on page 45, arrange the cubes into 13 rows. Rows 1, 3, 5, 7, 9, and 11 will have 6 cubes in each. Rows 2, 4, 6, 8, and 10 will have 7 cubes in each. Stitch the cubes together in each row, in the same manner that you stitched 2 diamonds together. Remember to orient the values in each cube the same way.

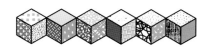

Rows 1, 3, 5, 7, 9, and 11

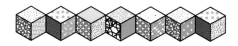

Rows 2, 4, 6, 8, and 10

2. Sew the rows together.
3. Press lightly and remove the basting threads and paper patches from all of the cubes, except the outside-edge diamonds. Press again.
4. Measure the quilt top, following the directions for mitred borders on pages 87–88. Cut 4"-wide strips from the lengthwise grain of the border fabric to match the measurements.
5. Place a border strip under the edge of each side of the pieced quilt top, centring each strip. Appliqué the folded edge of the outside-edge diamonds onto each border strip; try not to stitch through the paper. Do not stitch the cubes in the corners yet.

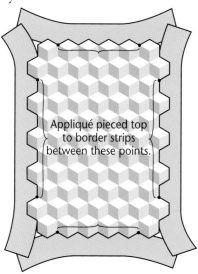

Appliqué pieced top to border strips between these points.

6. Mitre the corners of the border. Complete the appliqué of the 4 corners of the quilt top. Remove the remaining basting threads and paper patches.

## FINISHING THE QUILT

1. Layer the quilt top with batting and backing; baste.
2. Quilt as desired. Wendy outline-quilted ¼" inside each cube and continued the cube-shaped quilting pattern out into the border.
3. Bind the edges with 2½"-wide straight-grain strips of the binding print. (See pages 90–91.)

# Night Window

*Night Window by Judy Turner, 1994, Canberra, ACT, Australia, 54" x 50".*

A quilter whose work I really admire is Judy Turner. I consider her to be a true fibre artist. We have been fortunate to have her teach for us twice, and on both occasions, she inspired and motivated the students and taught them new skills—everything you can hope for from a visiting teacher!

Judy shares my love for floral fabrics, particularly the timeless favourite, Liberty of London Tana Lawn. The prints she uses range from tiny flowers to large blooms, such as poppies and roses. She often uses decorator fabrics.

The quilt includes the technique known as "broderie perse," where you cut floral motifs from large-scale floral prints and appliqué them in place. Search through your fabric collection for beautiful floral prints and have fun arranging your own vase of flowers!

THE GREAT BARRIER REEF, OFF THE NORTHEAST COAST OF AUSTRALIA, IS THE LONGEST CORAL REEF IN THE WORLD (1267 MILES) AND IS A PROTECTED MARINE PARK.

## MATERIALS: *44"-wide fabric*

⅔ yd. black solid for windowpanes
1¾ yds. light gray for window frame
⅛ yd. slightly darker gray for windowsill
1 yd. assorted large-scale floral prints for flowers*
12" x 12" square piece of tan print for vase
1½ yds. green print for border and binding
3 yds. for backing
54" x 58" piece of batting

*Be sure some have a black background.*

## CUTTING

*From the black solid fabric, cut:*
3 strips, each 8½" x 42"; crosscut into 12 rectangles, each 8½" x 10½", for Piece A (windowpanes)

*From the light gray fabric, cut:*
10 strips, each 2½" x 63" (lengthwise grain of fabric); crosscut into:
> 4 strips, each 2½" x 32½", for Piece D
> 2 strips, each 2½" x 42½", for Piece E
> 2 strips, each 2½" x 36½", for Piece F
> 1 strip, 2½" x 46½", for Piece G
> 1 strip, 2½" x 54½", for Piece H

4 strips, each 1½" x 34"; crosscut into:
> 8 strips, each 1½" x 8½", for Piece B
> 2 strips, each 1½" x 32½", for Piece C

*From crosswise grain of slightly darker gray fabric, cut:*
2 strips, each 1½" x 42", for Piece K

*From the lengthwise grain of the green fabric, cut:*
3 strips, each 4½" x 58½", for Pieces I and J (top and side borders)
1 strip, 5½" x 58½", for Piece L (bottom border)

## ASSEMBLING THE QUILT TOP

*Use accurate ¼"-wide seam allowances. Press all seams towards the darker fabric.*

1. Join Pieces A, B, and C as shown.

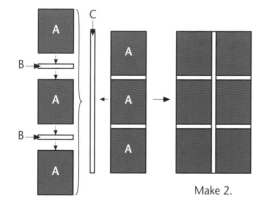

Make 2.

2. Sew 2 Piece D to the sides of the window section.

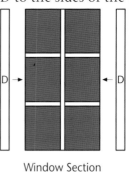

Window Section
Make 2.

3. Sew the 2 window sections together to make 1 window unit.

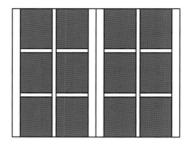

4. Join 2 Piece E to the window unit, then add 2 Piece F.

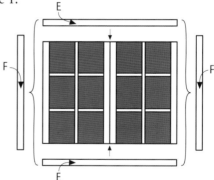

5. Sew Piece G to the top edge of the window.

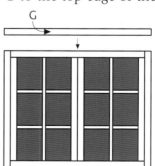

6. Mark the centre of the window and the centre of Piece H with pins. With right sides together, pin Piece H to the bottom edge, matching the centres. Sew Piece H in place, beginning and ending ¼" from the edge with a few backstitches. Judy used the wrong side of the fabric as the right side to create a sense of dimension for the windowsill. Do not trim the ends of Piece H that extend beyond the edges of the window.

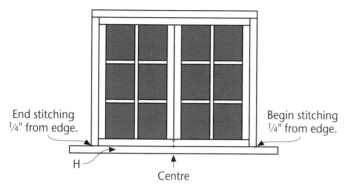

End stitching ¼" from edge.

Begin stitching ¼" from edge.

H

Centre

7. Refer to "Mitred Borders" on pages 87–88. Sew Piece J to the top of the window.
8. Sew Piece I to the sides of the window, mitring the corners where they join Piece J. At the bottom of Piece I, stop stitching at the same 2 points where you began and ended the seam in step 6.
9. Fold and press 13°-angle lines into each end of Piece H as shown. The outside point of the angles are 1¼" from the bottom of Piece H.

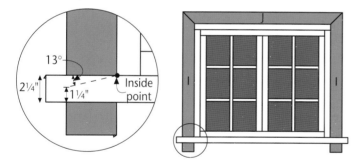

13°

2¼"

1¼"

Inside point

J

I

I

10. With right sides together, sew Piece H to Piece I on the crease line. Begin at the inside point and stitch to the outside point. Press the seams open and trim away excess fabric, leaving ¼"-wide seam allowances. Repeat with the remaining corner of Piece H.
11. Stitch Pieces K together, end to end. Press and trim length to 58½". Sew resulting Piece K to Piece L. Measure the width of the quilt top along the bottom edge of Piece H. Trim the KL unit to match that measurement. Join the resulting unit to the bottom edge of the windowsill.

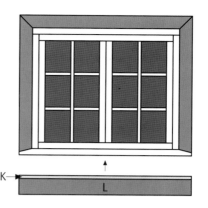

K

L

## APPLIQUÉING THE FLORAL ARRANGEMENT

1. Make a template of the vase, using the pattern on the pullout pattern insert. See "Making Templates" on page 84.
2. Trace around the template onto the right side of the vase fabric. Cut out the vase, adding a ¼"-wide seam allowance all around.
3. Pin the vase in place on the windowsill, slightly to one side of the centre. Appliqué by hand. Appliqué techniques begin on page 84.
4. From the assorted floral prints, cut out a variety of flowers (remembering to add a seam allowance all around) and arrange them around the vase. Be sure to use any trailing flowers or tall, fine stems that are printed on fabric with a black background because the background will blend into the black windows. The most successful arrangements contain a variety of shapes and colours.
5. Pin the flowers in place. When you are satisfied with your arrangement, appliqué them to the background. Judy appliquéd a fallen petal onto the windowsill.

## FINISHING THE QUILT

1. Layer the quilt top with batting and backing; baste.
2. Quilt as desired. Judy quilted in-the-ditch around all sections of the windowpanes and frames, vase, and flowers. She also quilted inside the vase.
3. Bind the edges with 2½"-wide straight-grain strips of the green fabric. (See pages 90–91.)

# Signatures

*Signatures by Beryl Hodges, 1994, Canberra, A.C.T., Australia, 38" x 38".*

We got to know Beryl Hodges at The Calico House some years ago. Shortly before she left Perth for Canberra, our nation's capital, Beryl taught for us in her warm and charming manner. We were sorry she had to go. As the wife of a senior army man, Beryl has been saying "Au revoir" to friends all over the world for many years.

When Beryl left Perth, her quilting group made her a delightful wall hanging. Each member made a block that included her own face and distinguishing feature— it depicted each friend so well.

The quilt is a perfect choice for creating a lasting memory of a special family occasion, a farewell gift, or simply a reminder of good times. Make it in plaids like this one or in pretty florals. Have everyone sign it and present it to a favourite person.

## MATERIALS: *44"-wide fabric*

Assorted scraps of plaids for blocks (or approximately ¾ yd.)
½ yd. light plaid for signature strips
¼ yd. plaid for inner border
¾ yd. plaid for outer border
¼ yd. plaid for outer border corner squares
1¼ yds. for backing
½ yd. plaid for binding
42" x 42" piece of batting

## CUTTING

Templates are on the pullout pattern insert.

*From the assorted scraps of plaid fabrics, cut:*
72 Template A (triangles)

*From the light fabric, cut:*
36 Template B (signature strips)

*From the inner border fabric, cut:*
4 strips, each 1½" x 42"

*From the outer border fabric, cut:*
4 strips, each 5" x 42"

*From the outer border corner-square fabric, cut:*
4 squares, each 5" x 5"

## MAKING THE BLOCKS

*Use ¼"-wide seam allowances.*

1. Piece 36 blocks as shown.

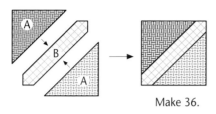

Make 36.

2. Collect signatures for each block. Signatures can be embroidered or written with a waterproof pen.

## ASSEMBLING THE QUILT TOP

1. Arrange the blocks into groups as shown. When you are pleased with the arrangement of colors, stitch the blocks together into groups of 4.

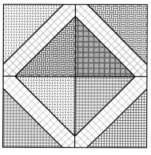

Make 5.          Make 4.

2. Sew the groups of blocks together into 3 rows of 3 groups each, making sure to match the seams between the groups. Refer to the colour photo.

3. Add the inner borders, measuring and cutting as directed for "Straight-Cut Borders" on pages 86–87.

4. Sew the outer borders to the quilt top, adding the corner squares. See "Borders with Corner Squares" on page 87.

## FINISHING THE QUILT

1. Layer quilt top with batting and backing; baste.
2. Quilt as desired.
3. Bind the edges with 3"-wide straight-grain strips of plaid fabric. (See pages 90–91.) Notice that Beryl used 2 different fabrics for her binding strips. Experiment and bind your quilt the way that suits you best!

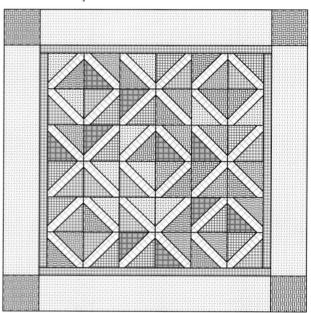

WESTERN AUSTRALIA IS THREE TIMES THE SIZE OF THE STATE OF TEXAS BUT HAS A POPULATION OF ONLY 1.7 MILLION.

# Stars & Hearts

*Stars & Hearts by Helen Ryan, 1994, Perth, Western Australia, 60½" x 60½".*

ROTTNEST ISLAND, WESTERN AUSTRALIA. PHOTO BY PHOTO INDEX.

*Busy people seem to achieve so much. A prime example is Helen Ryan, who is a full-time nursing sister and a qualified wool classer! (A wool classer sorts and grades wool immediately following shearing. Sometimes up to 1200 sheep are sheared in a single day.) She always manages to come up with new quilt designs, classes, and helps out in the shop when needed.*

*Helen designed the quilt on page 55 and its companion, the "Homeward Bound" quilt on page 60, which is almost half size. The placement of the Heart blocks in groups of four gives a visual effect of hearts on the move. Helen's work is detailed and precise, with each piece meeting accurately.*

## MATERIALS: *44"-wide fabric*

1½ yds. background for Heart blocks
1 yd. background for Star blocks in second border
¼ yd. each of 18 different medium to dark prints for Heart and Star blocks
1 yd. for first and thlird (narrow) borders
2 yds. for fourth (outer) border and binding
2¾ yds. for backing
50" x 50" piece of batting

AUSTRALIA IS THE WORLD'S LARGEST INHABITED ISLAND AND THE SMALLEST CONTINENT. IT IS ALSO THE LARGEST CONTINENT INHABITED BY ONE NATION AND IS THE LEAST POPULATED.

# Making the Blocks

## Heart Blocks

*Use ¼"-wide seam allowances. Assemble 2 Heart blocks from each fabric. When you are using a number of different fabrics, organize them by block so that you do not mix up the pieces. Finished block size: 5½" x 5½"*

*From Heart block background fabric, cut:*
5 strips, each 1¾" x 42"; crosscut into 114 squares, each 1¾" x 1¾", for A
3 strips, each 2¾" x 42"; crosscut into 36 squares, each 2¾" x 2¾", for B
7 strips, each 1¾" x 42"; crosscut into 36 rectangles, each 1¾" x 6", for C*
8 strips, each 1¾" x 42"; crosscut into 36 rectangles, each 1¾" x 7¼", for D*

*\*Depending on your fabric width after preshrinking, you may need to cut 1 or 2 more rectangles from your fabric.*

*From each of the 18 prints, cut:*
1 strip, 3¾" x 12"; crosscut into 2 rectangles, each 3¾" x 6", for G. You need a total of 36 rectangles.
1 strip, 2¾" x 8"; crosscut into 2 rectangles, each 2¾" x 3¾", for H. You need a total of 36 rectangles.

1. Draw a diagonal line from corner to corner on the wrong side of each 1¼" background square (A). Place a square on one end of a heart-fabric rectangle (H) as shown. Stitch on the marked line. Trim away excess, leaving a ¼"-wide seam allowance. Press seam towards the print fabric. Repeat with another square on the opposite end of the rectangle.

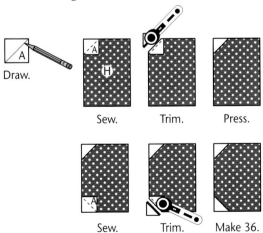
Draw. Sew. Trim. Press.
Sew. Trim. Make 36.

2. Repeat the same process as in step 1 above for heart-fabric rectangle (G).

Make 36.

3. Sew background square (B) and the units made in steps 1 and 2 together. Be sure to match the print fabrics within each heart.

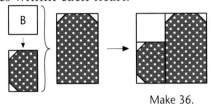
Make 36.

4. Sew background rectangles (C) and (D) in place. Note that on 24 blocks, the background rectangles are added at the bottom of the heart; and on 12 blocks, the rectangles are added at the top. Press seams towards the darker fabric.

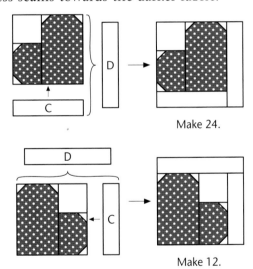
Make 24.

Make 12.

## Star Blocks

*Make 3 identical Star blocks from each of 16 different fabrics and 4 identical Star blocks from each of the other 2 fabrics, for a total of 56 Star blocks. Cut all strips from the crosswise grain of fabric. Use ¼"-wide seam allowances. Finished block size: 3" x 3".*

*From Star block background fabric, cut:*
7 strips, each 1¼" x 42"; crosscut into 224 squares, each 1¼" x 1¼", for A

11 strips, each 1¼" x 42"; crosscut into 224 rectangles, each 1¼" x 2", for B

*From each of 16 different prints, cut:*
1 strip, each 1¼" x 42"; crosscut into 24 squares, each 1¼" x 1¼", for C. You need a total of 384 squares.
1 strip, 2" x 7"; crosscut into 3 squares, each 2" x 2", for D. You need a total of 48 squares.

*From the remaining 2 prints, cut:*
2 strips, each 1¼" x 42"; crosscut into 32 squares, each 1¼" x 1¼", for C. You need a total of 64 squares.
1 strip, 2" x 9"; crosscut into 4 squares, each 2" x 2", for D. You need a total of 8 squares.

1. Draw a diagonal line from corner to corner on the wrong side of each 1¼" star-fabric square (C). Place a square on one end of a background rectangle (B) as shown on page 58. Stitch on the marked line. Trim away excess, leaving a ¼"-wide seam allowance. Press seam towards the print fabric. Repeat with another square on the opposite end of the rectangle.

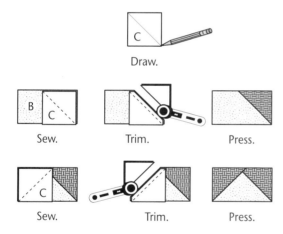

2. Sew the Star blocks together as shown. Be sure to match the print fabrics within each star. Press seams in opposite directions from row to row. Join the rows together to complete each block.

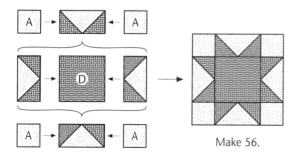

Make 56.

## ASSEMBLING THE QUILT TOP

1. Arrange the Heart blocks into groups of 4, orienting them as shown. Note that the 4 corner groups differ from the 4 side groups, and that the centre block is different. When you are pleased with the orientation of colours, sew the hearts together into groups of 4.

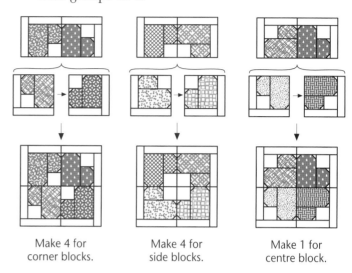

Make 4 for corner blocks.  Make 4 for side blocks.  Make 1 for centre block.

2. Referring to the quilt plan, sew the groups together into 3 rows of 3 groups each. Press the seams in opposite directions from row to row.
3. Sew the rows together, making sure to match the seams between groups.
4. Add the borders, measuring and cutting as directed for straight-cut borders on pages 86–87. Note that on this quilt, the top and bottom borders are added first, then the side borders.

### First Border

Measure the quilt top. From the crosswise grain of the first and third border fabric, cut 1½"-wide strips to match the measurements. Piece the strips as necessary, end to end, to make the required lengths. Press the seams open. Sew the top and bottom borders to the quilt top first, then add the side borders.

### Second Border (Stars)

Measure the quilt top, including the first border. Arrange the Star blocks into border strips. The top and bottom border strips each have 13 Star blocks, and the side border strips each have 15 Star blocks. Before stitching the blocks together, add spacer strips to each strip. From the Star block background fabric, cut 4 strips, each 2¼" x 3½", for spacer strips.

When you are pleased with the colour arrangement of the border strips, stitch the blocks together for the top and bottom border strips, adding a spacer strip to each end of the strips.

Spacer strip                                              Spacer strip

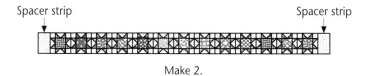

Make 2.

For the side border strips, stitch 15 blocks together, adding spacer strips between the last 2 Star blocks at each end of the strips as shown.

Spacer strip                                              Spacer strip

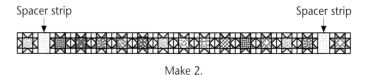

Make 2.

## Third Border

Measure the quilt top. From the crosswise grain of the first and third border fabric, cut 1½"-wide strips to match the measurements. Add the borders to the quilt top as you did for the first border.

## Fourth Border

Measure the quilt top. From the crosswise grain of the fourth border fabric, cut 5½"-wide strips to match the measurements. Add the borders to the quilt top as you did for the first and third borders.

## FINISHING THE QUILT

1. Layer the quilt top with batting and backing; baste.
2. Quilt as desired.
3. Bind the edges with 2¾"-wide straight-grain strips of the binding fabric. (See pages 90–91.)

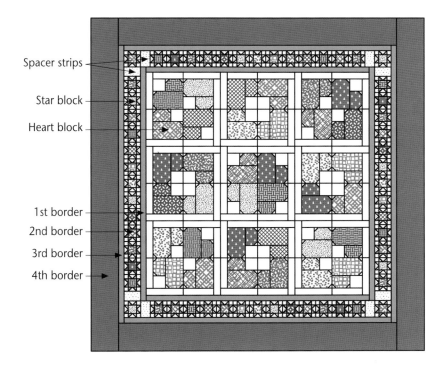

Spacer strips
Star block
Heart block
1st border
2nd border
3rd border
4th border

# Homeward Bound

Homeward Bound by Helen Ryan, 1994, Perth, Western Australia, 26" x 26". A smaller
variation of Helen's Stars & Hearts quilt includes an inner border of Flying Geese.

AYERS ROCK, OR ULURU (ITS ABORIGINAL NAME), IS A RED GRANITE MONOLITH IN THE CENTRE OF AUSTRALIA. ITS CIRCUMFERENCE IS 5.3 MILES.

*Helen's quilt is a smaller version of her Stars & Hearts quilt on page 55. While the hearts in the centre of the quilt are completed in the same manner as the larger quilt, she reduced their scale. Rather than make smaller Star blocks, which would have been very time-consuming and tedious, Helen made tiny Flying Geese blocks instead.*

*This quilt is made using the paper foundation-piecing method. The results are accurate, and you can complete the quilt in a relatively short period of time.*

## MATERIALS: *44"-wide fabric*

¼ yd. background for Heart blocks
¼ yd. background for Flying Geese blocks in second border
Assorted scraps of 18 different medium to dark prints for Heart and Flying Geese blocks*
¼ yd. for first and third (narrow) borders
¼ yd. for fourth (outer) border and binding
1 yd. for backing
30" x 30" piece of batting
37 copies of the Heart pattern for foundation piecing
13 copies of the Flying Geese pattern for foundation piecing

*Scraps should be at least 4" x 4".*

## MAKING THE BLOCKS

Use the patterns on the pullout pattern insert. Use accurate ¼"-wide seam allowances. All the marked lines on the paper foundation are the seam lines. All fabric pieces are positioned on the unmarked side of the paper. Attention to the straight grain of fabric is not necessary, as the pieces are relatively small and the paper foundation adds stability while you are stitching the seams. You will stitch the fabric pieces directly onto the paper foundations. Finger-press each piece open over the space it is to cover on the paper. Make sure that an adequate seam allowance extends into the adjacent areas. Add each in the numerical order indicated on the pattern, stitching on the seam line. When machine stitching fabric pieces on paper foundations, use a 90/14 Universal needle and set the stitch length to 14 to 18 stitches per inch. To reduce bulk, trim seam allowances to ⅛" to ³⁄₁₆" wide. Turn the block over, fold the foundation back out of the way, then trim.

## MAKING THE FOUNDATION COPIES

To prepare the paper foundations, photocopy the patterns. Because different copy machines may produce copies with a slight variance, always be sure to make all copies for each project on the same machine, from the original block in this book. Be sure there is a margin of 1" on each side of the block. It is a good idea to reduce the toner on the photocopier as the pattern lines can be transferred permanently onto your fabric with the iron.

Make 37 copies of the Heart block (1 for practice) and 13 of the Flying Geese strip (1 for practice).

## MAKING THE HEART BLOCKS

Finished block size: 2½" x 2½"

1. Follow the piecing sequence indicated by the numbers on the pattern. Place Piece 1, right side up, on the unmarked side of the paper. Make sure the edges of the fabric piece extend into the adjacent areas. Pin in place. Place Piece 2 on top of Piece 1, right sides together, along the joining seam line. Pin in place. Make sure both fabrics extend at least ¼" beyond the seam lines.
   Cut Pieces 1, 2, and 5 from the print fabrics. Pieces 3, 4, 6, 7, and 8 are cut from the background fabric. Organize the print fabrics by block so that you do not mix up the pieces.

Marked side of paper with first seam

Unmarked side of paper

2. Carefully turn the paper over so that the marked side of the paper faces up, holding the pieces of fabric in place. Pin in place on the marked side of the paper. Remove the pins from the unmarked side. Stitch on the line, through the layers of the paper and the 2 fabric pieces.

3. Finger-press Piece 2 over the area it is to cover on the paper foundation. Trim the excess fabric, being careful to leave a seam allowance that extends into the adjacent areas.

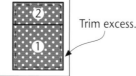

Trim excess.

Unmarked side of paper

4. Add Piece 3, placing it right sides together with Piece 2. Stitch, finger-press, and trim as you did before. Continue by adding Pieces 4–7 in the same manner until the design is complete.

5. For Piece 8, fold and finger-press a ¼"-wide seam on one side of a 1¼" x 1¼" square of background fabric. Place Piece 8 with right sides together on top of the foundation as shown. The folded edge of the piece should align with the seam line between Pieces 3 and 8. The bottom edge of Piece 8 should extend over Pieces 5 and 7 by ¼". Stitch Piece 8 in place on the seam line between Pieces 7 and 8, beginning at the point where Pieces 1, 2, and 5 intersect. Finger-press the piece over the foundation. Hand stitch the remaining seam between Pieces 3 and 8, using the blindstitch.

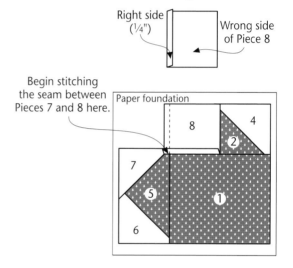

Make 36 blocks. Press the completed blocks with an iron.

6. Stitch around outside edge of each block between the solid design line and the dashed trim line.

7. Trim away excess fabric that extends outside the trim line of each block. Do not remove the paper foundation yet.

## MAKING THE FLYING GEESE BLOCKS

The Flying Geese blocks for the second border are made using the paper foundation-piecing method. Instead of making each block individually and then piecing them together into border strips, they are made in strips of 14 blocks.

1. The side borders each require 38 Flying Geese blocks; therefore, each side border requires 3 copies of the border-strip foundation. With a glue stick, paste 3 strips together, then trim away the excess number of Flying Geese blocks.

2. The top and bottom borders each require 41 Flying Geese blocks; therefore, they each require 3 copies of the border-strip foundation. Again, glue the strips together and trim away the excess number of Flying Geese blocks.

3. Follow steps 1–4 in "Making the Heart Blocks" on pages 61–62 to cover the paper foundation strips with fabrics. Cut Pieces 1, 4, 7, 10, etc. (the large triangles), from the print fabrics. Cut Pieces 2, 3, 5, 6, etc. (the small triangles), from the background fabric.

## ASSEMBLING THE QUILT TOP

*Use ¼"-wide seam allowances.*

1. From the background fabric, cut 6 strips, each 1" x 42"; crosscut into:
   18 rectangles, each 1" x 5½", for sides of Heart blocks
   6 strips, each 1" x 17¾", for horizontal sashing strips

2. Sew 1" x 5½" rectangles to Heart blocks as shown.

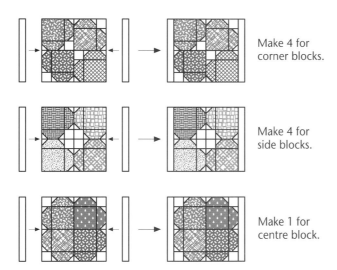

Make 4 for corner blocks.

Make 4 for side blocks.

Make 1 for centre block.

3. Arrange the Heart blocks into groups of 4, referring to the colour photo and to step 1, page 58, of the "Stars and Hearts" quilt. Note that the 4 corner groups differ from the 4 side groups and that the centre block is different. When you are pleased with the orientation of colours, sew the hearts together into groups of 4.

4. Sew the groups together into 3 rows of 3 groups each. Press the seams.

5. Sew the rows together, adding the background sashing strips to the tops and bottoms of each row as shown.

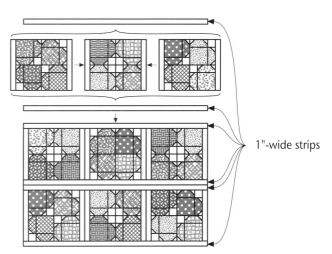

1"-wide strips

6. Add the borders, measuring and cutting as directed for straight-cut borders on pages 86–87.

### *First Border*

Measure the quilt top. From the crosswise grain of the first and third border fabric, cut 1"-wide strips to match the measurements. Piece the strips as necessary, end to end, to make the required lengths. Press the seams open. Sew the side borders to the quilt top first, then add the top and bottom borders as shown on page 87.

### *Second Border (Flying Geese)*

Sew the Flying Geese side border strips to the quilt top first, then add the top and bottom border strips.

### *Third Border*

Measure the quilt top. From the crosswise grain of the first and third border fabric, cut 1"-wide strips to match the measurements. Add the borders to the quilt top as you did for the first border.

### *Fourth Border*

Measure the quilt top. From the crosswise grain of the fourth border fabric, cut 3"-wide strips to match the measurements. Add the borders to the quilt top as you did for the first and third borders.

## FINISHING THE QUILT

1. Layer quilt top with batting and backing; baste.
2. Quilt as desired.
3. Bind the edges with 1¼"-wide straight-grain strips of the binding fabric. Helen recommends preparing single-fold binding. *Do not* fold the binding strip in half lengthwise before sewing the binding to the quilt as shown on page 91; in the final step, turn the raw edge under ¼" and blindstitch in place.

# Aussie Sweet Treats
## FOR MORNING TEA

*We always look forward to morning tea when a staff member brings along some home cooking.*
*So we thought we would include some genuine Aussie recipes for you.*

## LAMINGTONS

*My dear mother-in-law, Mary Brazier, gave me this recipe for an old Australian favourite, Lamingtons. These tea cakes are often made for fund-raising drives and are sold by the dozens. Mary's mother, Mrs. Clare Burt, was the state president of the Country Women's Association (C.W.A.) for Western Australia in the 1930s. She wrote in the foreword of the first edition of the C.W.A.'s cookbook, "Variety, the very spice of life, which gives it all its flavour." How very true!*

### Sponge

| | |
|---|---|
| ½ lb. of butter (2 sticks) | 1 tsp. baking soda |
| 1½ c. sugar | 2 tsp. cream of tartar |
| 3 to 4 drops vanilla extract | 3 c. flour |
| 4 eggs | 1 c. milk |

1. Preheat oven to 350°F. Butter and flour a 9" x 6" baking pan.
2. Whisk the butter, sugar, and vanilla until light and fluffy.
3. Beat the eggs, baking soda, and cream of tartar together until they form stiff peaks.
4. Fold the egg mixture into the butter mixture.
5. Sift ¼ cup of the flour over the mixture and fold it in. Fold in ⅛ cup of the milk. Repeat until all of the flour and milk has been added and the batter is smooth.
6. Pour the batter into the baking pan. Bake for 30 to 35 minutes. Allow the cake to cool slightly before removing it from the pan. Let it cool completely on a wire rack. If possible store the cake until the next day, then ice it.

### Soft Chocolate Icing

| | |
|---|---|
| 4 tbsp. boiling water | 4 c. confectioners' sugar |
| 1 tbsp. butter | 3 to 4 drops vanilla extract |
| 3 tbsp. cocoa | 4 to 5 c. shredded coconut |

1. Combine the boiling water, butter, and cocoa in a medium saucepan. Stir over low heat until blended. Heat for 1 minute.
2. Remove the pan from the heat. Add the sugar gradually, beating it until the mixture is smooth; it will be runny. Stir in vanilla.
3. Cut the cake into 3" x 3" squares. Place a cake square on a two-pronged fork, and dip it in the icing. Cover all the sides of the square with icing. Next, roll the square in the coconut to completely cover it, then place it on a wire rack to set. Repeat with the remaining cake squares. If the icing thickens, stir in a few drops of boiling water. If the icing cools, stir it over low heat for a few minutes.

# ANZAC Biscuits

*How appropriate I am writing this recipe on April 25, ANZAC (Australian and New Zealand Army Corps) Day, our national day of remembrance for our fallen soldiers.*

*My husband's grandfather, Colonel Brazier, led the 10th Light Horse Brigade from Western Australia to Turkey in 1915. It was on the shores of Gallipoli that a dreadful battle took place, despite Colonel Brazier's warning to his superiors in Britain that a battle would be a mistake.*

*These biscuits, or cookies, are delightful with Earl Grey tea. This recipe was provided by Jan Houghton.*

1 c. rolled oats
1 c. flour, sifted
1 c. sugar
¾ c. shredded coconut
8 tbsp. butter

1 tbsp. golden syrup
   (or maple syrup)
1½ tsp. baking soda
2 tbsp. boiling water

1. Preheat oven to 425°F.
2. In a medium bowl, combine the rolled oats, flour, sugar, and coconut.
3. In a small saucepan, combine butter and syrup. Stir over low heat until butter is melted.
4. Mix baking soda with boiling water and add to melted butter mixture. Stir into dry ingredients.
5. Drop the batter by dessert spoonfuls* onto a greased baking sheet, about 2" apart. (A dessert spoon is smaller than a tablespoon and larger than a teaspoon.) Bake 15 to 20 minutes. Allow the biscuits to cool slightly on the trays before transferring them to wire racks to cool completely. Makes approximately 36 biscuits.

# Pavlova

*This delicious dessert is another Australian favourite. West Australians like to believe that its origins are local. After the famous Russian ballerina Anna Pavlova danced in Perth, the chef at the Esplanade Hotel created this recipe in her honour. Whatever is the true tale, it certainly tastes wonderful! This recipe is from Jenny Burke.*

## Meringue

4 egg whites
Pinch of salt
1 c. superfine sugar

1 tsp. vinegar
½ tsp. vanilla extract
1 level dessert spoon cornstarch*

1. Preheat oven to 400°F.
2. Beat egg whites with salt for 5 to 6 minutes. Gradually beat in the sugar, vinegar, and vanilla. Beat until stiff peaks form. Sift the cornstarch over the mixture and fold in lightly.
3. Line a flat tray with foil. Pile the mixture (about the size of a dinner plate) onto lined tray. Make a shallow well in the surface (to accommodate the topping later).
4. If you have an electric oven, place the tray with the meringue in the oven and immediately lower the temperature to 250°F. Bake for 1½ hours. If you have a gas oven, place the tray with the meringue in the oven and bake for 10 minutes at 350°F, then lower the temperature to 250°F and bake for 1 hour.
5. Allow meringue to cool, then fill with topping.

***NOTE:*** If you live in a high altitude, we have been told that the meringue may not rise properly!

## Topping

Fill the meringue with whipped cream. Decorate with fresh, sliced bananas, passion fruit, strawberries, and kiwi fruit.

*\*A dessert spoon is smaller than a tablespoon and larger than a teaspoon.*

# Wagon Doll

*Wagon Doll by Vicki Lauritsen, 1994, Geraldton, Western Australia, 22" tall.*

*Vicki is another favourite country customer, teacher, and friend, who loves to design and make wonderful soft toys. She lives in the coastal town of Geraldton, which is 312 miles north of Perth.*

*Vicki designed the Wagon Doll after reading a library book about children's toys on the wagon trains. Not very Australian, you may say, but rag dolls were universal in their different forms. My mother, as one of eleven children growing up on a farm, had only wooden pegs for dolls. She and her sisters cut the "legs" off short on some to make baby dolls and knew each peg intimately as a particular character. How different it is today!*

*With her buttoned-on scrap hair and smiling face, this doll makes an ideal playmate for a child. In an age of plastic, adult-looking dolls, it is comforting to think a doll like this can be carted around and loved to bits.*

*Playing with their Wagon Dolls in a wonderful Moreton Bay fig tree are (from top) Miffy Mullen, Caitlin Slatter, and Alexandra Readhead.*

## MATERIALS: *44"-wide fabric*

½ yd. homespun or muslin for doll's body
¾ yd. print for dress
½ yd. stripe or check for bloomers
⅛ yd. each of 6 to 8 different fabrics for doll's hair
16-oz. bag of polyester fiberfill for stuffing
25 to 30 buttons, each 1" to 1½" diameter for doll's hair
Embroidery threads: brown for eyes, red for lips, pink for nose, colours to match dress and bloomers
Button-and-carpet thread to match fabric for doll's body
2 small buttons for dress bodice
4 snaps for back closure of dress
Template plastic
Water-soluble marking pen
Large-eyed needle for stitching "hair" buttons
Darning or tapestry needle
Wooden spoon or chopstick to stuff doll

## BEFORE YOU BEGIN

The patterns are on the pullout pattern insert. Make plastic templates as described on page 84 for the doll head/body, arms, legs, and dress bodice. Using a water-soluble marking pen, mark the arm and leg placement on the body, and the stuffing lines on the arm and leg pieces. Mark the facial features, too. Be sure to test your pen on a scrap of the fabric first to make sure you can remove the marks.

## MAKING THE DOLL

Adjust the stitch length on your machine to 20 stitches per inch, or sew the seam twice, making 2 rows of stitching right next to each other. This makes the seams sturdy to accommodate the pressure from the stuffing.

Dollmakers use a number of tools for stuffing. The long handle of a wooden spoon, a chopstick, or the eraser end of an unsharpened pencil all work well.

1. Cut the head/body, arms, and legs from the homespun or muslin. Mark the placement of the arms and legs. Mark the eyes and mouth.
2. With arms right sides together, stitch around the outer edges of each pair of arm pieces. Stitch ¼" from the raw edges, leaving the top edge open for stuffing. Clip curved edges and between the thumb and first finger. Turn right side out. Stuff each arm to the stuffing line (elbow). Stitch across the elbow. Do not stuff above the elbows.

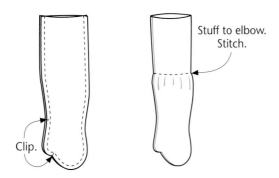

Stuff to elbow.
Stitch.

Clip.

3. With legs right sides together, stitch around the outer edges of each pair of leg pieces. Stitch ¼" from the raw edges, leaving the top edge open for stuffing. Clip curved edges and turn right side out. Stuff each leg to the stuffing line (knee). Stitch across the knee. Be sure each foot faces forward. Do not stuff above the knees.

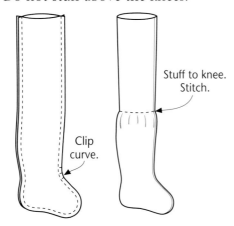

Stuff to knee.
Stitch.

Clip curve.

4. Place the arms on the right side of one of the head/body pieces. Make sure the thumbs point upward. Baste into place.

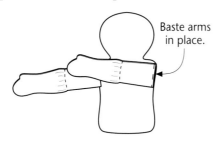

Baste arms in place.

5. With right sides together, place the second head/body piece on top of the first. Stitch ¼" from the raw edges, leaving the bottom edge open for inserting the legs and stuffing. Clip the curved edges of the neck and trim the seam allowances to ⅛" wide. Turn right side out.

Clips

Leave bottom edge open.

6. Tuck the legs about ½" into the bottom edge of the body. Make sure the legs are the same length and that both feet point forward. Pin in place to the back side of the body only. Sew the legs in place.

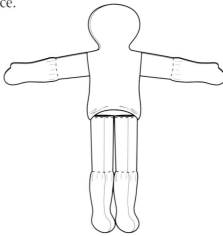

7. Firmly stuff the head and body. Turn under the seam allowances and stitch the bottom edges together with a ladder stitch, using button-and-carpet thread.

### To do the ladder stitch:

1. Secure the thread in the seam allowance so it doesn't show.
2. Take a stitch across the opening into the other side. Move the needle back to the opposite side and take another stitch. Make sure the seam allowance rolls inside the seam.
3. Make 3 to 4 stitches, going back and forth across the opening.
4. Pull the thread to start closing the opening. Make 3 to 4 more stitches, then pull the thread up. Continue stitching until the opening is closed. Knot the thread, close to the last stitch; then run

the thread a needle's length through the stuffing. Bring the needle back to the surface and clip the thread at the surface.

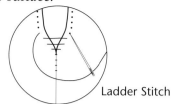

Ladder Stitch

5. Thread a large-eyed needle with a length of button-and-carpet thread. Knot the two ends together, creating a double strand. Sew 12 or 13 buttons on the seam line across the top of the doll's head, from "ear" to "ear." Leave a small space between the buttons. Sew the buttons on loosely (so that there is space to tie the hair strips on later), but securely, stitching between the buttons with small stitches. Sew the remaining buttons in place, in the same manner, covering the back of the doll's head.

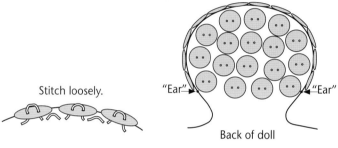

Stitch loosely.

"Ear"          "Ear"

Back of doll

## Helpful Hints

*To give the fabric an aged look, spray the body, arms, and legs with cold tea after the body has been stuffed and the buttons for the hair have been sewn on. Pour the tea into a plastic spray bottle. Hang the doll's body on a line and spritz the tea all over the surface. Let it dry thoroughly. Spray again for a darker look.*

# EMBROIDERING THE FACE

*Embroidery stitches are on page 89.*

1. Embroider the eyes with 3 strands of brown embroidery thread, using a satin stitch.
2. Embroider the mouth with 3 strands of red embroidery thread, using a stem stitch.
3. Embroider the nose with 3 strands of pink embroidery thread, using small straight stitches.

# MAKING THE CLOTHES

### Bloomers

1. From the striped or checked fabric, cut a 14½" x 16" rectangle. Fold the rectangle in half, with right sides matching the two 16"-long edges. Stitch the 16"-long edges together, using a ¼"-wide seam allowance. Press so that the seam is on one side.

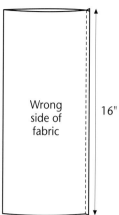

Wrong side of fabric          16"

2. Mark the centre of the crotch 10" from the bottom edge and 3" from the folded edge. Beginning at the bottom edge and using small stitches (20 stitches/inch), stitch up to the centre along a line that is 3¼" from the folded edge. Then sew across for ½", turn, and sew back to the bottom edge.

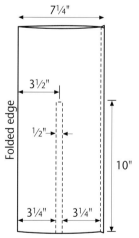

7¼"

3½"

Folded edge

½"

10"

3¼"     3¼"

3. Cut between the lines of stitching and clip into the corners. Turn the bloomers right side out.

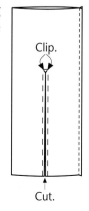

Clip.

Cut.

4. Turn under and press a ¼"-wide hem in each bloomer leg. Turn under and press an additional ¼"-wide hem. Machine stitch close to the folded edge of the hem. Press. At the top edge (waist), turn under ½" and press. With a darning or tapestry needle and 6 strands of embroidery thread, use small running stitches to sew around the waist and each leg. Do not knot the thread at the beginning or end of the stitching. Leave long tails of thread. Pull up the threads to gather the edges. Tie a double bow in each. Trim the tails of thread as desired.

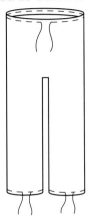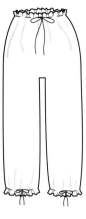

## Dress

1. *From the print fabric, cut:*
   1 bodice front, 1 bodice back, and 1 bodice back reversed, using the plastic templates
   1 strip, 15" x 42", for dress skirt
   2 squares, each 11" x 11", for sleeve
   1 bias strip, 1¼" x 13", for neckline bias binding
2. Place the bodice front and the two back pieces right sides together. Stitch the shoulder seams. Press seams open.

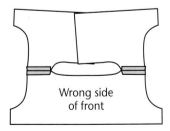

Wrong side of front

3. With right sides together and raw edges aligned, baste the bias strip to the neckline, ¼" inside the raw edge. Leave ½" overlapping at each end. Machine stitch into place and clip the curves almost to the seam line.

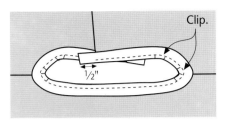

Clip.

½"

4. Fold the bias strip in half and in half again and hand stitch in place to the wrong side of the neckline.
5. Turn under and press a ½"-wide hem on each sleeve. Turn under and press an additional ½"-wide hem. Machine stitch halfway between the folded edges of the hem. On the opposite edge of each sleeve, sew a row of running stitches ½" away from the raw edge for gathering. Place a pin in the centre.

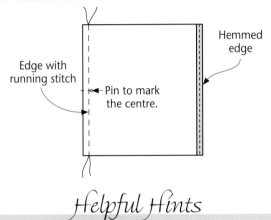

Edge with running stitch

Pin to mark the centre.

Hemmed edge

## Helpful Hints

*To make running stitches for gathering the edges of the doll's clothing, set the stitch length on your machine for long basting stitches. Always leave "tails" where you begin and end a row of basting stitches, to use when you gather the edge.*

6. With right sides together, place the sleeves on the bodice, matching the pin with the shoulder seam. Pull up the thread, gathering the edges to fit the armholes. Make sure the gathering is even. Stitch the sleeves in place.

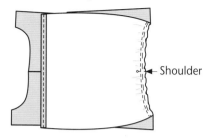

7. Sew the underarm seams of the sleeves and bodice. Sew running stitches in the hem of each sleeve as for the bloomers and gather to fit.

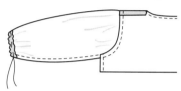

8. At one of the long edges of the 15" x 42" print strip, turn under and press a ½"-wide hem. Turn under and press an additional ½"-wide hem. Machine stitch close to the folded edge of the hem. On the opposite edge, sew 2 rows of running stitches ⅛" and ¼" from the raw edge. Place a pin in the centre.

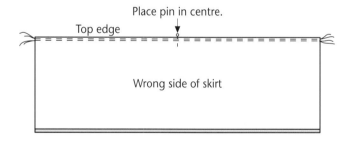

Place pin in centre.

Top edge

Wrong side of skirt

9. With right sides together, place the skirt on the bodice, matching the centre of the skirt with the centre of the bodice front. Pull up the threads, gathering the skirt to fit the bodice. Make sure the gathering is even. Stitch the skirt in place.

10. Trim the excess neckline bias on the back of the dress so that it is even with the edge of the bodice. At each back edge of the dress, turn under and press ⅛". Turn and press an additional ¼" and machine stitch. Stitch the snaps in place on the finished edges.

11. Hem the skirt by hand.

12. Using 6 strands of embroidery thread, sew the 2 small buttons to the front of the dress bodice. Leave small tails of thread.

## MAKING THE DOLL'S HAIR

1. From each of the fabrics for the hair, tear 4 to 5 strips, each ¾" x 42". Trim away all the long and loose threads to tidy up the strips. Do not cut the strips into smaller pieces.

2. With 2 strips at a time, tie them around the first button at the "ear" position. Make a tight knot, then trim the strips, leaving 3" tails. Take 2 more strips and tie them around the same button; again make a tight knot and trim the strips. Repeat the process on the next button until 4 strips are tied onto each of the buttons and the doll has a full head of hair. Tidy up the doll's hair by trimming the ends at a 45° angle.

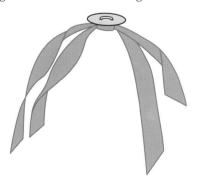

# The Secret Garden Smocked Bag

Secret Garden Smocked Bag designed and stitched by Margaret Herzfeld, 1994, Perth, Western Australia, 18" x 20". Margaret made the tote bag, then adapted the pattern to make an eyeglasses case and a needle case. Directions are given in this book for the tote bag.

CANBERRA, A.C.T. PHOTO BY BETTY METZ.

*I* made a special request to That Patchwork Place to include this smocked bag in our book, because Margaret Herzfeld has been teaching for us since day one. Margaret says her inspiration for this piece was a Charles Robinson illustration from a 1946 edition of Frances Hodgeson Burnett's book **The Secret Garden.** Margaret also makes exquisite smocked dresses for us, using her own intricate designs. These classic clothes always look lovely on children for special occasions.

The 17" x 19" bag on page 72 is a useful sewing tote. Or, instead of making a bag with the smocked and embroidered panel, frame it to hang on the wall, or make it into a pillow. Adapt the design and make a spectacle case and needle case for delightful accessories to give as gifts or to keep.

## MATERIALS: *44"-wide fabric*

¼ yd. of cream-coloured solid for smocked panel
24" x 42" print for front and back of bag
20" x 42" dark green for frame, top binding, and handles
18" x 42" light green for lining
20" x 36" piece of batting
8" x 34" piece of light or medium-weight fusible interfacing
Embroidery threads in light, medium, and dark pinks, yellow, 5 to 6 different greens, white, 2 different purples, 2 different blues, and a light brown

## BEFORE YOU BEGIN

Read all of the directions before beginning. Choose embroidery threads to match or complement your fabrics. For those of you who enjoy silk-ribbon embroidery, this design would look stunning done that way.

GREEN AND GOLD ARE AUSTRALIA'S NATIONAL COLOURS, THE WATTLE IS OUR NATIONAL FLOWER, AND THE KANGAROO IS OUR NATIONAL ANIMAL.

## Smocked and Embroidered Panel

1. From the cream-coloured solid fabric, cut an 8" x 42" strip.
2. Pleat 19 rows, using a Sally Stanley 24-row pleater and following the manufacturer's instructions. Tie the pleats off at a 10" width.
3. Back smock 19 rows of cable stitches by hand. Back smocking holds the pleats so the front is more stable, thereby making embroidery easier. The pleated panel should be 8" x 10".
4. Using the embroidery pattern on the pullout pattern insert, centre the design on the pleated panel. On the front side of the smocked panel, lightly draw with a pencil around the designs and around the outside edges of embroidery area.
5. Referring to the pattern, embroider the designs on the front of the smocked panel. The numbers on the embroidery design indicate recommended stitches. The Embroidery Stitch Chart on page 76 lists the numbers from the design, colours, and name of the stitch. Directions for the embroidery stitches are on page 89.
6. Carefully remove pleating threads after embroidery is complete. Do not remove the back smocking stitches.

## Making the Bag

*Use ¼"-wide seam allowances except where noted.*
1. Measure the smocked panel and trim so that the outside edges measure 7¼" x 9½". You need to leave a ¼"-wide seam allowance all around the embroidered area.
2. From the dark green fabric, cut:
   2 strips, each 1½" x 7¼", for the frame on the sides of the smocked panel
   2 strips, each 1½" x 11½", for the frame on the top and bottom of the smocked panel
3. With right sides together, stitch the frame strips to the right and left sides of the smocked panel.

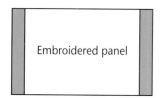

4. Stitch the top and bottom frame strips in place. Trim all sides of the frame to 1" wide.

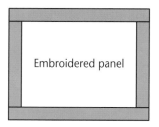

5. From the print fabric, cut:
   2 strips, each 4" x 8¾", for side borders
   1 strip, 6¾" x 18", for top border
   1 strip, 5½" x 18", for bottom border
   1 piece, 18" x 20", for back of bag
6. With right sides together, stitch the side borders in place.

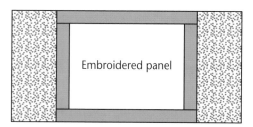

7. From the batting, cut 2 pieces, each 18" x 20". Place the front of the bag on one of the pieces of batting, 5" from the bottom. Pin, then baste around the outer edges. Set your sewing-machine stitch length for long stitches. Quilt-in-the-ditch (see page 88) in the seam that joins the smocked panel to the frame. Then quilt-in-the-ditch in the seam that joins the frame to the border.

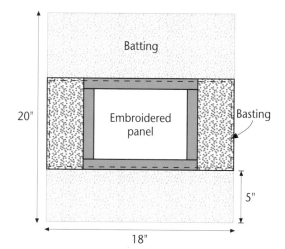

8. With right sides together, stitch the top and bottom borders in place. Flip the borders over onto the batting. The front of the bag is completed!

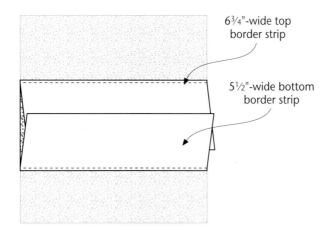

6¾"-wide top border strip

5½"-wide bottom border strip

9. Place the 18" x 20" piece of print fabric for bag back on the remaining piece of batting. Align the edges so that they match. Baste layers together.

10. With right sides together, sew the front and back together along the sides and bottom, using ½"-wide seam allowances. Clip the corners at a 45° angle, close to the stitched corner. Turn right side out and press.

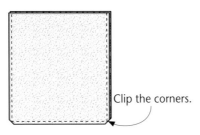

Clip the corners.

11. To make the lining, cut a 17½" x 39½" rectangle from your lining fabric. Fold the rectangle in half, right sides together, as shown. Sew the sides together, using ¼"-wide seam allowances. Press.

Fold

12. Place the lining inside the bag with wrong sides together. Baste the lining in place to the top edge.

13. From the dark green fabric, cut a 4" x 36" strip.

14. With right sides together, place the binding on the outside of the bag, 1" from the top edge (not the inside). Refer to "Attaching the Binding" on page 91 for beginning and ending binding. Using a ½"-wide seam allowance, sew the binding strip to the bag. Turn the bag inside out.

15. From the fusible interfacing, cut 2 strips, each 4" x 34". Iron an interfacing strip to the wrong side of each of the 2 handle strips.

16. Fold the handle strips in half lengthwise, right sides together. Turn strips right side out. Press the handles so that the seam is centred on one side of the handle. The side with the seam will be the wrong side of the handle.

17. With right sides together, pin one end of one handle to the inside of the bag, positioning it 3½" from the side. Pin the other end of the handle in the same manner, 3½" from the other side. Be sure the ends of the handles are placed ½" inside the seam that joined the binding strip to the bag. Sew the handles in place, in the same seam line as the binding. Stitch twice. Repeat with the other handle.

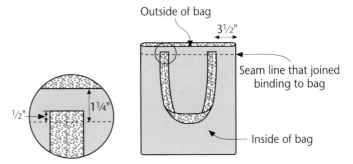

Outside of bag

3½"

Seam line that joined binding to bag

½"

1¼"

Inside of bag

18. Fold the binding over the raw edges of the top of the bag to the inside of the bag. Turn the raw edge under ½" and blindstitch in place.

19. Stitch the handles to the binding as shown, using a blind stitch. Turn the bag right side out.

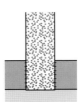

# EMBROIDERY STITCH CHART

| Area | Motif | | Stitch | No. of Strands | Colour |
|---|---|---|---|---|---|
| 1 | Roses | Petals | Bullion | 3 | 3 shades pink |
| | | Centre | French knot | 3 | pink |
| | | Leaves | Lazy daisy | 2 | 2 shades light green |
| | Tree | Trunk | Bullion (long)* | 3 | light brown |
| | | Branches | Stem | 3 | light brown |
| | Butterfly Bodies | | Bullion | 3 | light green |
| | | Wing outline | Lazy daisy (long)* | 3 | dark blue |
| | | Middle wing | Double lazy daisy | 3 | light blue |
| | | Centre wing | French knot | 3 | purple |
| | | Antennae | Pistil | 3 | light blue |
| 2 | Daisies | Petals | Lazy daisy | 3 | white |
| | | Centres | 3 French knots | 3 | yellow |
| | | Stems | Straight | 3 | medium green |
| | | Leaves | Lazy daisy | 3 | medium green |
| | Forget-Me-Nots | | French knot | 3 | light blue |
| | | Leaves | Straight and lazy daisy | 2 | light green |
| 3 | Lavender blooms | | Bullion | 3 | 2 purples |
| | | Stems | Fly | 2 | light green |
| 4 | Daffodils | | Lazy daisy* | 3 | yellow |
| | | Stems | Lazy daisy (long) | 2 | light green |
| 5 | Cornflowers | | French knots | 3 | dark blue |
| | | Leaves | Lazy daisy | 2 | medium green |
| | Daisies | Petals | Lazy daisy | 3 | white |
| | | Centres | 3 French knots | 3 | yellow |
| | | Stems | Straight | 3 | medium green |
| | | Leaves | Lazy daisy | 3 | medium green |
| | Foxgloves | | Lazy daisy | 3 | variety of pinks |
| | | Stems | Stem | 3 | medium and dark green |
| | | Leaves | Double lazy daisy | 3 | medium and dark green |
| 6 | Ground | | Smocked outline stitch | 3 | 6 greens |

*The long bullion stitch used for the tree trunk is made, then couched in place. The butterfly wing outline is a long, loose lazy daisy stitch that is tacked down in 2 places rather than 1 place. For the daffodil flowers, angle the stitches to form the petals, then satin stitch the ends together to form the calyx.*

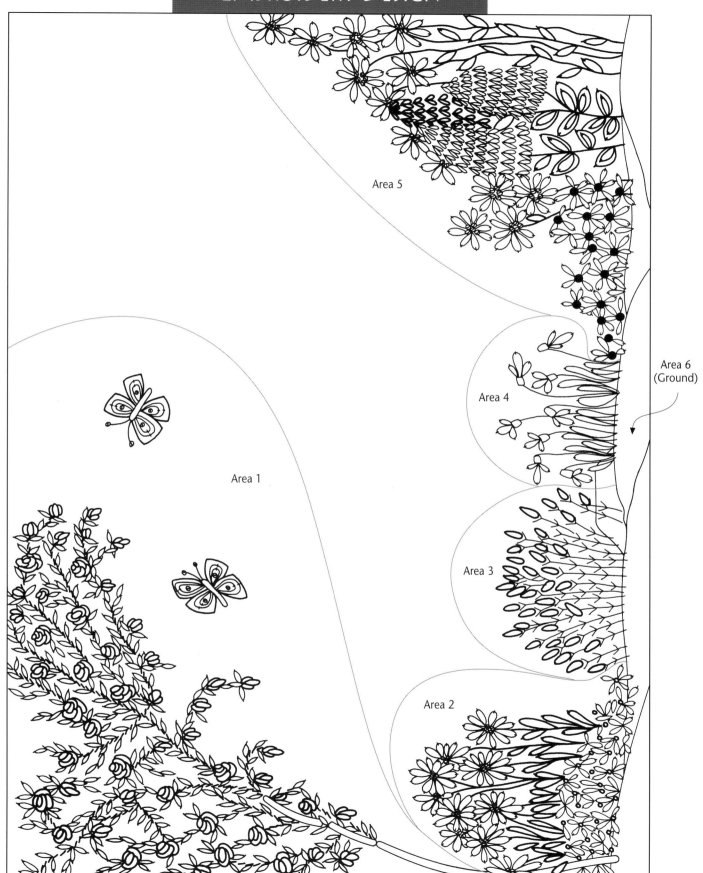

Area 5

Area 6
(Ground)

Area 1

Area 4

Area 3

Area 2

# Molly & Moe,
## the Sweetheart Bears

*Molly & Moe, the Sweetheart Bears by Lynette LeRoy, 1994, Perth, Western Australia, 12" tall.*

*A*s we photographed the bears, seated on their little twig bench, they really seemed to be looking at the camera! It sounds silly, I know, but something about their expressions made them come to life.

Our bear creator, Lynette LeRoy, has been a devoted collector and bear maker for years. Now making her own designs under the label "Mulga Bill Bears," Lynette will only part with them if she is convinced they are going to a good home. Bears seem to have that effect on people, and, perhaps, the world would be a better place if everyone had a bear to love.

Make a single bear for yourself, or the pair would be a delightful engagement or wedding present, or a gift to twins. The only difference between Moe's pattern and Molly's pattern is the shape of the arms.

PHOTO BY PHOTO INDEX.

## MATERIALS *(for one bear)*

¼ yd. low-pile plush fur or mohair
4" x 6" piece of felt for paws, footpads, and nose
Ten 1½" (38mm) hardboard discs for joints*
Ten ¾" (2cm) washers with ¼"- (7mm) diameter hole for joints*
Five 2½" (6cm) cotter pins for joints*
Two ⅜" (10mm) acrylic or glass eyes or coat buttons**
Embroidery thread for nose and mouth
Button-and-carpet thread for closing openings
16-oz. bag of polyester fiberfill for stuffing
1 cup plastic pellets for bear and dollmaking
Needle-nose pliers
Long quilt (straight) pins
Long doll needles
Long-handled wooden spoon or chopstick to stuff bear

*These items may be purchased in hardware stores. Many craft stores and shops that specialize in doll- and bear-making supplies also carry these parts or have sets of joints specifically made for bears. You may substitute bear joints for the parts listed here; just be sure that you purchase joints that are appropriate for 12"-tall bears.
**If you are making the bear for a young child, use safety eyes or embroider the eyes instead of attaching buttons or acrylic or glass eyes.

## BEFORE YOU BEGIN

1. The patterns are on the pullout pattern insert. Make plastic templates as described on page 84 for all bear pieces. Mark the arrow lines on the templates because they indicate the direction of the plush-fur nap. Note that the arms for the boy bear and the girl bear are different.

   To determine the nap, run your hand in each direction across the surface. If the surface is smooth and has less resistance to your touch, that is nap. If the surface is rough or has resistance, that is "against the nap."

2. Note on the patterns that the footpads and paw pads are to be cut from felt. All the other pieces are cut from the plush fur. Lay the templates on the wrong side of the fur. To minimize wasting fur, cut the largest pattern pieces first. Cut out the ears last. Be sure to orient nap-of-fur arrow lines correctly. Using a pencil, trace around the templates and cut out the pieces. Use the tip of your scissors to cut only the backing (not the fur) as you cut out each pattern piece. Remember to reverse the template when required for some of the pattern pieces. Cut pieces one at a time from plush fur; do not stack layers as you would with woven fabrics.

3. When pinning and sewing plush, always smooth the fur to the inside as you work to avoid catching fur in the seam. Long quilter's pins are useful. Begin with the head, pinning two sides together. To avoid sewing a lopsided face, baste all head pieces together before sewing them together.

4. After stitching seams, clip or notch the corners and curved edges to ensure the correct shape and smooth curves when the bear is turned right side out. Use sharp scissors and clip to within a few threads of the stitched seam, but *do not cut into the seam.*

## MAKING THE BEAR

*Use ¼"-wide seam allowances.*

1. With right sides together and raw edges aligned, stitch the head and head reversed pieces together along the chin seam, from point A (nose) to point B (neck) as shown.

2. With right sides together, pin the head gusset in place, aligning point A (the centre of the head gusset) with the chin seam that you stitched in step 1. Sew around the top of the nose, from point C to point D.

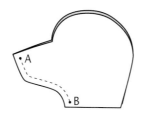

3. Pin the edges of the gusset to the head between points D and E and sew the pieces together between the 2 points. Pin the remaining edge of the gusset to the head between points C and F, then sew between the 2 points. Clip curves. Turn right side out.

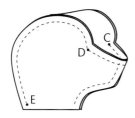
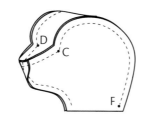

4. With right sides together, stitch the felt paw pad to the inside arm at the wrist line. Repeat with the other arm.

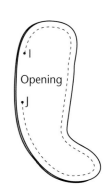

5. With right sides together, pin the inner arm to the outer arm. Sew the pieces together between points I and J. Be sure to leave the seam open where indicated. Clip curves. Turn right side out. Repeat with the other arm.

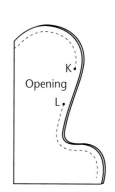

6. Fold leg piece in half along centre line so that the right sides are together. Pin in place, then stitch together, leaving open between points K and L. Leave the seam open where indicated. Do not stitch the bottom of the foot. Repeat with the other leg.

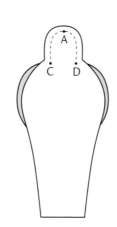

7. With right sides together, pin felt footpad into the opening at the bottom of the foot. Baste in place, then sew the pieces together. Turn right side out.

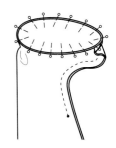

8. With right sides together, pin the two front body pieces together. Sew the pieces together between points M and N, to complete the tummy seam.

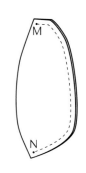

9. Sew the two back pieces, stitching from point O to P to complete the centre back seam. Make sure to leave open where indicated.

10. With right sides together, pin the fronts and backs together at the side seams. Match the seams at the bottom edges of the two pieces. Sew each side seam from the neck down to the bottom edge. Sew the seam again so that the seam will be sturdy and can accommodate the pressure from stuffing the bear. Turn right side out through the back opening.

11. With right sides together, stitch the two ear pieces together. Do not stitch between points U and V. Turn right side out. Tuck the seam allowances into the ear, then hand stitch the opening closed. Repeat for the other ear.

You have now made all of the bear's body parts! Next, you will assemble them into your own huggable bear!

## Finishing the Head

1. If you have selected safety eyes, they must be placed on the bear's head prior to stuffing the bear. Referring to the photo on page 78, mark the location of the eyes and make a small hole with a knitting needle or snip a tiny opening in the marked area. Lynette placed them just inside the seam lines that join the head gusset and the head.

   Place the eye shanks from the right side through to the wrong side of the head and place the safety back on the shank. Make sure the back is securely on the shank.

   If you plan to embroider eyes or add buttons for eyes, go to step 2.

2. Begin stuffing the head, filling the nose first. To stuff the head evenly, use your hand to shape the snout; to fill the body, add small amounts of stuffing gradually. Make sure you round out the seams. Work up towards the neck opening, filling the neck section last. Do not fill all the way to the top so that the fabric extends above the stuffing.

3. With button-and-carpet thread, sew a running stitch all around the neck, ¼" inside the raw edge. Leave tails at each end.

4. Organize the joints for your bear as shown. You should have 5 sets of joints—for the head, arms, and legs.

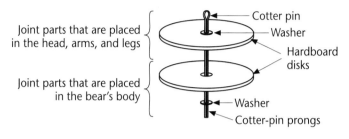

**Joint Parts**

5. Place a joint in the base of the head as shown. Pull up the thread tails to gather the neck and close the fabric around the cotter pin. The cotter-pin prongs should protrude from the head. Be sure to sew the edges together firmly around the cotter pin. Tie a double knot, then clip the excess thread.

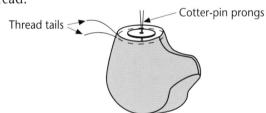

6. Pin the ears to the head, positioning them where you like them. Make sure they are even. Lynette attached them to the head, curving the ears so that they "cup" slightly. Stitch the ears in place with button-and-carpet thread, making closely spaced, small stitches.

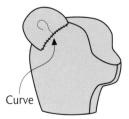

7. If you haven't already attached the eyes, mark their location. Using a doll needle, make a small hole in each location to accommodate the shank on the back of the eyes.

8. Thread a long doll needle with a length of button-and-carpet thread. Bring the two ends together and knot them together, creating a double strand. Stitch each eye in place, pulling the thread firmly so that the shank is recessed into the hole that you created with the doll pin. Bring the needle and thread out to the surface at the base of the neck. Make sure the eyes are even. Knot the thread ends together and hide them.

9. Join the bear's head to its body. Push the cotter-pin prongs inside the top of the body where all the seam lines that join the back and front body pieces intersect. Run the prongs of the cotter pin through the centre of a hardboard disk, then a washer. Refer to the "Joint Parts" illustration on page 81.

   Using your needle-nose pliers, tightly curl the prongs of the cotter pin, forming what is known as a "crown joint." This creates a secure joint.

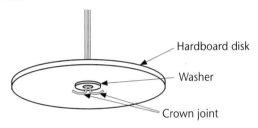

Hardboard disk

Washer

Crown joint

10. From the scraps of felt, cut out a nose. Pin the nose in place. Glue it to the snout with craft glue. Allow it to dry.

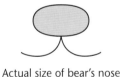

Actual size of bear's nose

11. Using satin stitches, embroider the nose with a colour that matches the felt or another colour that you like. Use a long doll needle. Begin stitching by burying the knot about a needle's length away from the nose. Cover the felt nose with closely spaced, even satin stitches. This gives the nose a three-dimensional look and a slightly padded feel. The more times you stitch over the area, the more dimension the nose will have.

12. After completing the nose, extend the stitches to make the mouth, referring to the pattern. Knot the thread and bury the thread in the stuffing, about a needle's length away from the mouth.

## ATTACHING THE ARMS AND LEGS

1. Make sure the joint marks are visible on the wrong side of the bear's fur (arms, legs, and the back body pieces). With a knitting needle or the point of a pencil, make a small hole in the fur backing, in each of the joint marks. Place a joint inside an arm, referring to the "Joint Parts" illustration on page 81. Push the cotter-pin prongs through the joint hole in the arm, then push it through the appropriate joint hole in the body. Next, run the cotter-pin prongs through a hardboard disk, then a washer. Make a crown joint to secure the joint. Refer to step 9 at left. Repeat with the other arm, then attach the legs in the same manner.

   *Be sure that you join the right arm and leg to the right side of the body and the left arm and leg to the left side of the body!*

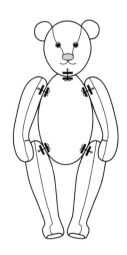

## COMPLETING THE BEAR

1. Stuff the bear's body in the same manner as the head. Beginning with small amounts of stuffing, fill the feet, then work your way up until the legs are evenly filled. Pour 1 cup of pellets into the bear's tummy, then fill the rest of the tummy with stuffing until the body is firm. Stitch the opening closed with button-and-carpet thread, using a ladder stitch. (See pages 68–69.)

2. Firmly stuff the arms and legs. Stitch the openings closed as you did for the body.

Now give your bear a big hug, a name, and a nice place to live for the rest of his or her life!

# Quiltmaking Basics

## Making Accurate Seams

Accurate and consistent ¼"-wide seams must be maintained to get the desired finished size of the quilt blocks. Use a ¼" quiltmaking presser foot on your sewing machine or mark an accurate ¼"-wide sewing guide on your machine. Use a ruler or graph paper with a ¼" grid to determine the measurement and mark the guide. Place masking tape or moleskin on the plate of the machine. Set the stitch length at 10 to 12 stitches per inch. Change your needle frequently. Backstitching is not necessary where seams will cross each other.

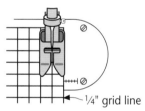

¼" grid line

Use ¼" graph paper
to mark an accurate seam guide.

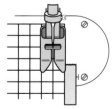

Put masking tape or moleskin
in front of needle along edge
of graph paper to guide fabric.

## Chain Piecing & Matching Seams

*Be sure to maintain an accurate ¼"-wide seam allowance.*

1. When sewing squares together, use a pin to mark the top (or end) square of each vertical row so that you don't mix them up while sewing. Pick up the top two squares of each row and place them right sides together. Feed them through the machine one after the other in a chain.

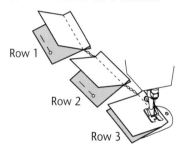

Row 1
Row 2
Row 3

2. Remove the chain of squares from the machine but do not cut them apart. Add the third square to the bottom of each row and stitch them to the pairs that you stitched together in step 1.

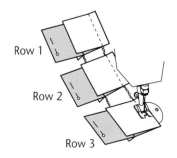

Row 1
Row 2
Row 3

Continue adding squares, but do not clip the threads until after you have finished.

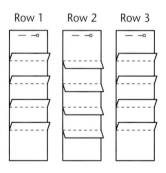

3. Press the seams to one side, alternating the direction from row to row. Press seams in the odd-numbered rows up, and the seams in the even-numbered rows down.

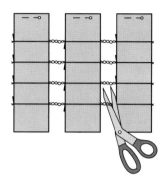

Row 1    Row 2    Row 3

4. Pin the rows, right sides together. Be sure to pin each intersection before stitching to ensure matched seams. Notice that there will be a seam allowance on each side where the seam lines come together. These are opposing seam allowances, which occur because the seam allowances were pressed in opposite directions from row to row. The seams fit together, and the

bulk of the layers is distributed evenly at the seam intersections.

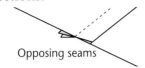

Opposing seams

5. To avoid warped rows or a curved quilt top when stitching the rows together, alternate the direction where you begin stitching from row to row.

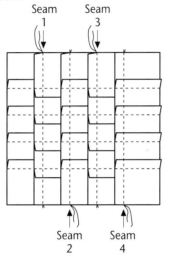

Seam 1    Seam 3

Seam 2    Seam 4

# Making Templates

Make sturdy templates from the patterns or templates provided, in one of the following ways. Templates for piecing will include seam allowances. Templates for appliqué will not include seam allowances. Be sure to mark the pattern name, piece number, and the grain-line arrow (if needed) on each template.

Lay a piece of paper over the pattern page and trace the designs with a sharp pencil or fine-tip permanent pen, then glue the entire page onto a sheet of cardboard. Cut out the individual pieces to use as templates.

Trace the pattern pieces onto template plastic with a sharp pencil or fine-tip permanent pen, then cut out the pieces.

# Appliqué Techniques

## CUTTING THE APPLIQUÉS

Place the template face up on the right side of the fabric. Trace around the template with a lead or chalk pencil. The drawn line marks the turned-under stitching edge. Cut out the pieces, adding a ¼"-wide seam allowance all around. Some quilters prefer to add a scant ¼"-wide seam allowance. A scant ¼"-wide seam allowance is ³⁄₁₆" to ¼" wide or 2 threads short of ¼".

See also "Freezer-Paper Appliqué" on page 85.

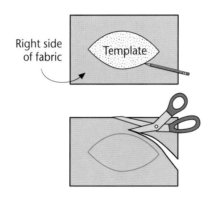

Right side of fabric

Template

## APPLIQUÉ STITCH

The blind stitch or traditional appliqué stitch may be used for sewing all appliqué shapes in place.

1. Tie a knot in a single strand of thread that is approximately 18" long.
2. Hide the knot by slipping the needle into the seam allowance from the wrong side of the appliqué piece; bring the needle out on the fold line.
3. Work from right to left if you are right-handed, or from left to right if you are left-handed.

4. Start the first stitch by moving the needle straight off the appliqué, inserting the needle into the background fabric. Let the needle travel under the background fabric parallel to the edge of the appliqué, bringing it up about ⅛" away along the pattern line.
5. As you bring the needle up, pierce the edge of the appliqué piece, catching only one or two threads of the folded edge.
6. Move the needle straight off the appliqué into the background fabric. Let your needle travel under the background, bringing it up about ⅛" away, again catching the edge of the appliqué.

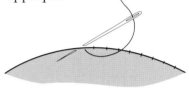

Appliqué stitch

7. Give the thread a slight tug and continue to stitch around the appliqué piece.
8. To end your stitching, pull the needle through to the wrong side. Behind the appliqué piece, take two small stitches, making knots by taking your needle through the loops. Check the right side to see if thread "shadows" through your background. If it does, take one more small stitch on the back side to direct the tail of the thread under the appliqué fabric so that it won't show through to the right side.

## Helpful Hints

*No matter which method you choose to appliqué, to get smoothly curved edges, clip inside points and the seam allowance on inside curves. Clip up to, but not across, the stitching line.*

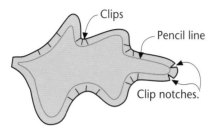

Clips

Pencil line

Clip notches.

*For sharp outside points, turn the point in towards the centre of the appliqué piece, then fold the two sides in to form the point. Trim excess seam allowance to eliminate bulky points.*

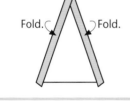

Fold.  Fold.

### FREEZER-PAPER APPLIQUÉ

1. Trace the appliqué design onto the paper (non-shiny) side of the freezer paper and cut out the shape exactly on the traced line.
2. Using the freezer-paper shape as your pattern, cut out the fabric piece, adding ¼"-wide seam allowances all around.

Wrong side of fabric

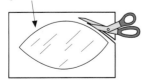

3. Lay the freezer paper on top of the wrong side of the fabric piece, with the shiny side of the freezer paper face up.

---

4. Fold the ¼"-wide seam allowance of fabric over the edge of the freezer-paper shape. Clip curves and corners to ease the fabric smoothly over the freezer-paper shape. Use the tip of your iron to press the seam allowances to the shiny side of the freezer paper. The heat will fuse the edges of the fabric in place, creating a perfect appliqué shape.

5. Do not remove the freezer paper yet. Pin the shape to the background or press in place with a warm iron and appliqué in place.
6. Cut out the fabric behind the appliqué piece, leaving a ¼"-wide seam allowance. Remove the freezer paper. Press.

Leave ¼" seam allowance all around.

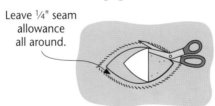

Cut away background fabric only.

### BASTED APPLIQUÉ

1. Using a plastic or cardboard template, trace around the shape on the wrong side of the fabric.
2. Cut the fabric shape a scant ¼" (³⁄₁₆" to ¼") from the drawn line.
3. Fold the seam allowance on the drawn line and baste around the edges, using long running stitches.
4. Pin or baste the shape to the background, then appliqué in place. Basting around the

---

edges of the pieces takes a little longer, but it makes the actual appliqué process go faster.

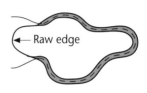

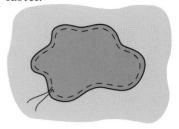

Raw edge

### NEEDLE-TURN APPLIQUÉ

1. Using a plastic or cardboard template, trace around the shape on the right side of the appliqué fabric.
2. Cut out the fabric shape, adding a scant ¼" (³⁄₁₆" to ¼") from the drawn line all around.
3. Pin or baste the shape to the background fabric.
4. Starting on a straight edge, use the tip of your needle to turn under the seam allowance, about ½" at a time. Hold the turned seam allowance firmly between the thumb and first finger of your left hand (reverse if you are left-handed) as you stitch the appliqué to the background. Use a longer needle, such as a "Sharp" or milliner's needle, to help you turn the seam allowance under neatly.

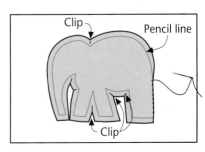

Clip

Pencil line

Clip

*It is not necessary to turn under the seam allowances of edges that will be covered by other appliqué shapes.*

## APPLIQUÉ STEMS OR ANIMAL LEGS

Some of the patterns in this book require prepared bias strips to create stems, plant stalks, or animal legs for appliqué. Use metal or heat-resistant nylon press bars, or make a pressing template the finished width of the stem from card stock. Make long "tubes" of stems and cut them to the required lengths as you appliqué.

1. Cut bias strips the finished width of the stem, plus ½" for seam allowances.
2. Place the fabric on your ironing board, right side down. Centre the press bar or template on the fabric. Press one side of the fabric over the bar, then the other to make a "tube." Remove the bar.

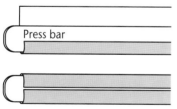

Press bar

3. Cut the required stem lengths from the stem "tube" as you need them. Place the folded edges of the stem on the penciled placement line of your background fabric. Stitch in place. If the block has curved stems, stitch the inside curve in place first and then the outside curve.

## APPLIQUÉ CIRCLES

1. Cut circle templates the exact size of the finished circle from heavy paper, such as a manila file folder.
2. Trace around the template onto the fabric. Cut the circles from the fabric, adding ¼" around the edge of the template.
3. Sew with a small running stitch around the fabric circle. Keep the stitches within the seam allowance but not too close to the edge.

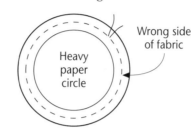

Wrong side of fabric

Heavy paper circle

4. Place the paper template in the centre of the wrong side of the fabric circle. Pull the thread ends to draw the seam allowance in around the template.

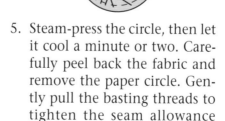

5. Steam-press the circle, then let it cool a minute or two. Carefully peel back the fabric and remove the paper circle. Gently pull the basting threads to tighten the seam allowance and make it lie flat.
6. Pin the circle to the background and appliqué with tiny stitches.

## Squaring Up the Blocks

After completing your blocks, it is important to square them up.

Use a large square or rectangular ruler to carefully measure each block. Make sure all the blocks are the desired finished size plus an extra ¼" all around for seam allowances. Trim away any excess fabric.

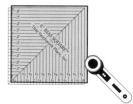

## Adding Borders

### STRAIGHT-CUT BORDERS

1. Measure the length of the quilt top through the centre. Cut border strips to that measurement, piecing as necessary. If you have already cut strips, trim them to that measurement. Mark the centre of the quilt edges and the border strips. Pin the borders to the sides of the quilt top, matching the centre marks and ends and easing as necessary. Sew the border strips in place. Press seams towards the border.

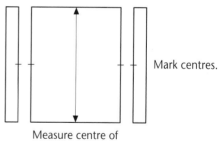

Mark centres.

Measure centre of quilt, top to bottom.

2. Measure the width of the quilt top through the centre, including the side borders just added. Cut border strips to that measurement, piecing as necessary. If you have already cut strips, trim them to that measurement. Mark the centre of the quilt edges and the border strips. Pin the borders to the top and bottom edges

of the quilt top, matching the centre marks and ends and easing as necessary. Sew the border strips in place. Press seams towards the border.

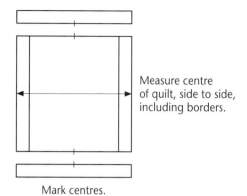

Measure centre of quilt, side to side, including borders.

Mark centres.

## BORDERS WITH CORNER SQUARES

1. Measure the width and length of the quilt top through the centre. Cut border strips to those measurements, piecing as necessary. Mark the centre of the quilt edges and the border strips. Pin the side borders to the sides of the quilt top, matching the centre marks and ends and easing as necessary. Sew the border strips in place. Press seams towards the border.

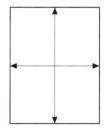

2. Cut corner squares of the required size (the cut width of the border strips). Sew one corner square to each end of the remaining two border strips; press seams towards the border strips. Pin the border strips to the top and bottom edges of the quilt top. Match centres, seams between the border strip and corner

square, and ends, easing as necessary. Sew the border strips in place. Press seams towards the border.

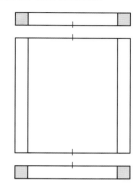

## MITRED BORDERS

1. Estimate the finished outside dimensions of your quilt, including borders. Border strips should be cut to this length plus at least ½" for seam allowances; it is safer to add 3" to 4" to give yourself some leeway. For example, if your quilt measures 45½" x 50½" across the centre and you want a 5"-wide finished border, your quilt will measure 55" x 60" after the border is attached.

*NOTE:* If your quilt has multiple borders, sew the individual strips together and treat the resulting unit as a single border strip.

2. Mark the centre of the quilt edges and the border strips.
3. Measure the length and width of the quilt top across the centre. Note the measurements.
4. Place a pin at each end of the side border strips to mark the length of the quilt top. Repeat with top and bottom borders.

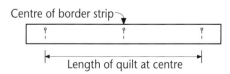

Centre of border strip

Length of quilt at centre

5. Pin the borders to the quilt top, matching the centres. Line up the pins at either end of the border strip with the edges of the quilt. Sew in place, beginning and ending the stitching ¼" from the raw edges of the quilt top. Repeat with the remaining borders.

Stitching begins ¼" from corner of quilt top.

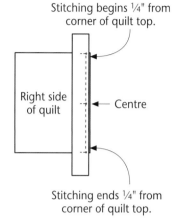

Right side of quilt

Centre

Stitching ends ¼" from corner of quilt top.

6. Lay the first corner to be mitred on your ironing board. Fold under one border strip at a 45° angle to the other strip. Press and pin.

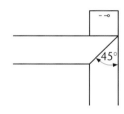

45°

7. Fold the quilt with right sides together, lining up the edges of the border. If necessary, use a ruler to draw a pencil line on the crease to make the line more visible. Sew on the pressed crease, stitching from the corner to the outside edge.

Pressed crease

Stitch from the corner to the outside edge.

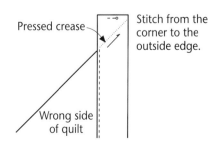

Wrong side of quilt

8. Press the seam open and trim away excess borders strips, leaving a ¼"-wide seam allowance.
9. Repeat with remaining corners.

## *Marking the Quilting Design*

Press your quilt top. Mark the quilting design on the quilt top, whether you hand or machine quilt, unless you are stitching in-the-ditch, outlining the design ¼" way from the seams, or stitching a grid of straight lines, using ¼"-wide masking tape as a guide. Don't leave tape on a quilt top for an extended period of time because the tape may leave a sticky residue.

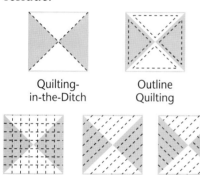

Quilting-in-the-Ditch          Outline Quilting

Crosshatched Grid          Diagonal Grids

- To quilt in-the-ditch, place the stitches in the valley created next to the seam. Stitch on the side that does not have the seam allowance under it.
- To outline a design, stitch ¼" away from the seam inside each shape. You can quilt without marking the line or use ¼"-wide masking tape.
- To mark a grid or pattern of lines that are ¼" apart, use ¼"-wide masking tape in 15" to 18" lengths. Place strips of tape on the quilt top and quilt next to the edge of the tape. Remove the tape when stitch-

ing is complete. Reuse the tape to mark another area.

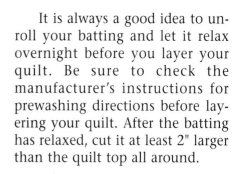

Masking tape

To mark other quilting designs, use a stencil or trace a design onto the quilt top, using a light table, before it is layered with the batting and backing. Use stencils to mark repeated designs. Marking pens and pencils are available in a variety of colors. Always draw the lines lightly and always test markers on a scrap of fabric to make sure the lines can be removed.

## *Layering the Quilt*

Make your quilt backing at least 3" to 4" larger than the quilt top all around. For a large quilt, you will usually need to sew two or three lengths of fabric together to make a backing of the required size. Trim away the selvages before piecing the lengths together. Press the backing seams open to make quilting easier. Save leftover fabric for another quilt project. If you find fabric wider than 44", you may not need as many lengths to make the backing.

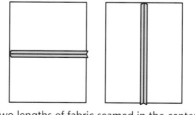

Two lengths of fabric seamed in the center

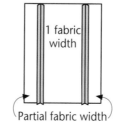

1 fabric width

Partial fabric width

It is always a good idea to unroll your batting and let it relax overnight before you layer your quilt. Be sure to check the manufacturer's instructions for prewashing directions before layering your quilt. After the batting has relaxed, cut it at least 2" larger than the quilt top all around.

1. Spread the backing, wrong side up, on a flat surface. Anchor it with pins or masking tape. Be careful not to stretch the backing out of shape.
2. Spread the batting over the backing, smoothing out any wrinkles.
3. Place the pressed quilt top on top of the batting. Smooth out any wrinkles and make sure the edges of the quilt top are parallel to the edges of the backing.
4. Starting in the centre, baste with needle and thread and work diagonally to each corner. Continue basting in a grid of horizontal and vertical lines 6" to 8" apart. Finish by basting around the edges. When you are quilting, you may find that you will need to remove the basting from the edges in order to smooth out wrinkles that occur during quilting. Remove the masking tape after you have completed the basting.

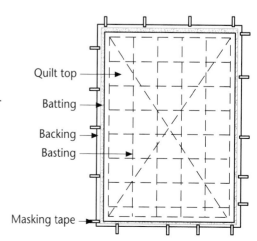

Quilt top

Batting

Backing

Basting

Masking tape

# Embroidery Stitches

You can use these embroidery stitches to embellish the blocks in your quilts.

Embroidery needles come in different sizes. Use a needle with an eye that will accommodate the number of strands of embroidery floss you plan to use. Carefully pull the end of the floss from the skein and cut a length no longer than 18". Separate the desired number of strands from the length that you just cut. Knot the strands together at the ends that have just been cut from the skein.

**Running Stitch**

**Pistil Stitch**

**Herringbone Stitch**

**Detached Chain or Lazy Daisy Stitch**

**Double Lazy Daisy**

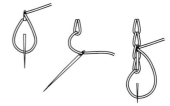

**Chain Stitch**

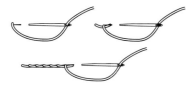

**Stem Stitch**

**Buttonhole Stitch**

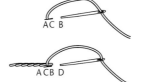

AC B

ACB D

**Outline Stitch**

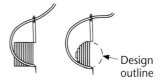

Design outline

**Satin Stitch**

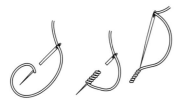

**Bullion Stitch**

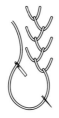

**Feather Stitch**

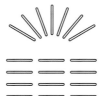

**Straight Stitch**

A          B

**Fly Stitch**

1. Start with centre of rose: 2 parallel bullions of 8–10 wraps each.

2. Add 5 bullions around the centre with 12 wraps each.

3. Add 6 bullions with 15 wraps each.

**Bullion Roses**

**French Knot**

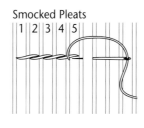

Smocked Pleats

1 2 3 4 5

**Smocked Outline Stitch**

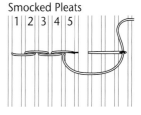

Smocked Pleats

1 2 3 4 5

**Cable Stitch for Back Smocking**

# Hand Quilting

For many quilters, hand quilting not only adds dimension to a quilt, but its very process is a relaxing pastime. All you need are short quilting needles known as "Betweens," quilting thread, and a thimble. Most quilters use a hoop or frame to support the quilt while they work.

1. Thread the needle with a single strand of quilting thread, about 18" long. Make a small, single knot at the end of the thread.
2. Insert the needle in the top layer about 1" from where you want to start stitching. Pull the needle out at the point where quilting will begin and gently pull the thread until the knot pops through the fabric and into the batting.
3. Take small, evenly spaced stitches through all three quilt layers.
4. Rock the needle up and down through all layers until you have three or four stitches on the needle. Place your other hand underneath the quilt so you can feel the point of the needle with the tip of your finger when a stitch is taken.
5. To end a line of quilting, make a small knot close to the last stitch. Then backstitch, running the thread a needle's length through the batting. Gently pull the thread until the knot pops into the batting; clip the thread at the quilt's surface.

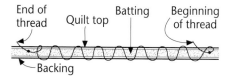

# Machine Quilting

Quilting by machine not only takes less time but is more durable for quilts that will have heavy use. Practice machine quilting on pieces of scrap fabric and batting layered together.

For straight-line quilting, a walking foot helps feed the layers through the machine without shifting or puckering. (See quilting designs on page 88.)

For free-motion quilting, lower the feed dogs and use a darning foot, which allows you to follow the curves of your pattern, or create stippling.

Walking foot          Darning foot

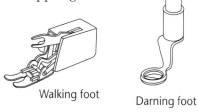

Free-Motion Quilting

If you plan to machine quilt, you may baste the layers with #2 rustproof safety pins. Place pins about 6" to 8" apart, away from the area you plan to quilt.

For more techniques on hand quilting, refer to *Loving Stitches* by Jeana Kimball. Maurine Noble's *Machine Quilting Made Easy* is a comprehensive source of machine-quilting techniques. Both books are published by That Patchwork Place.

# Binding

## STRAIGHT-GRAIN BINDING

Many of the projects in this book require straight-grain binding. To make this kind of binding, cut strips from the binding fabric to match the width required for the project. Cut enough strips to go around the perimeter of the quilt, plus 10" for seams and corners in a mitred fold. To make one long continuous piece, join the strips at right angles and stitch across the corner as shown. Trim excess fabric.

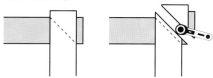

Joining Straight-Cut Strips

## BIAS BINDING

To make bias binding, fold one corner of your piece of fabric to its opposite corner, creating a right triangle. Crease the fabric on the fold. Use the resulting 45° crease as a guide to cut strips along the true bias. For a ⅜"-wide finished double-fold binding, cut 2½"-wide strips, measuring from the first bias cut. Using diagonal seams, stitch the ends together to make one long continuous piece. Press seams open.

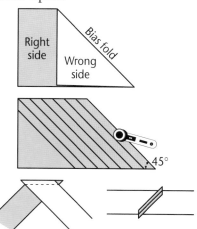

## ATTACHING THE BINDING

1. Trim the batting and backing even with the quilt-top edges, unless instructed otherwise in the quilt directions.
2. Fold the strip in half lengthwise, wrong sides together, and press.

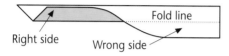

Right side — Fold line — Wrong side

3. At one end of the strip, turn under ¼" at a 45° angle and press.

Fold line

4. Start on one side of the quilt, a few inches from one of the corners. Sew along the edge, using a ¼"-wide seam allowance and ending ¼" from the next corner; backstitch.

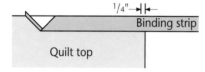

¼"
Binding strip
Quilt top

5. Fold the binding straight up, then bring it straight down onto itself. Begin sewing at the edge, backstitching to secure, and end ¼" from the next corner. Repeat with remaining edges and corners.

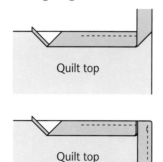

Quilt top

Quilt top

6. When you reach the point where you started, cut off excess binding at a 45° angle, leaving 1" to overlap the folded end of the binding. Tuck the binding end into the fold and finish the seam.

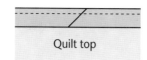

Quilt top

7. Turn the binding to the back of the quilt and blindstitch in place, covering the machine stitching. Tuck the corners to form a mitre and blindstitch.

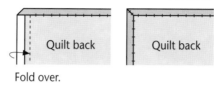

Quilt back    Quilt back

Fold over.

## BINDING WITH MEASURED STRIPS

Use this binding method if the outside edges of your quilt need to be eased to the binding so that their finished measurements conform to the measurement at the quilt's centre. Straight-grain binding strips work best for this type of binding.

1. Bind the long edges of the quilt first. Measure the length of the quilt at the centre, raw edge to raw edge. Do not measure the outer edges of the quilt! The edges of a quilt often measure longer than the quilt centre due to stretching during construction. The edges may even be two different lengths.
2. From your long strip of binding, cut two pieces of binding to the lengthwise centre measurement. Working from the right side of the quilt, pin the binding strips to the long edges of the quilt, matching the ends and centres and easing the edges to fit as necessary. Using an even-feed foot, sew the binding to the quilt with a ⅜"-wide seam. Fold the binding to the back, over the raw edges of the quilt (or, in the case of the "Light & Shade Liberty" quilt on page 16, over the edge of the batting); the folded edge of the binding should just cover the machine-stitching line. Blindstitch the binding in place, making sure your stitches do not show on the front of the quilt.

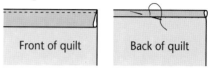

Front of quilt    Back of quilt

3. Prepare and sew the binding strips for the shorter edges of the quilt. Measure the width of the quilt at the centre, outside edge to outside edge. From the long strip of binding, cut two pieces to that measurement plus 1". Pin these strips to the short edges of the quilt, matching the centres and leaving ½" of the binding extending at each end. Ease the edges to fit as necessary. Sew the binding to the quilt with a ⅜"-wide seam.
4. Fold the extended portion of the binding strips down over the bound edges. Bring the binding to the back and blindstitch in place as before.

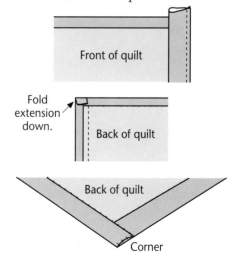

Front of quilt

Fold extension down.

Back of quilt

Back of quilt

Corner

# Meet the Author

Owning a quilt shop and even writing a book such as this one are a little like conducting an orchestra. Surrounded by talented people, you enable them to come together to display their skills and talents and provide pleasure for others.

I believe that owning a quilt shop is so much more than "just running a business." It is stimulating, challenging, and multi-faceted, as well as constant and exhausting. Some days, I contemplate selling up and spending more quality time with family and friends, reading, writing, gardening in a leisurely manner, or perhaps even sewing again! On all the other days, I value the creative and mental stimulation that the shop provides and realize how much more I achieve when I am really busy.

After twelve years of retailing, I am aware that one of the pitfalls of owning a shop is that it can end up owning you, but fortunately, the positives are plentiful, too. Making lifelong friends with staff and customers and having the opportunity to meet constant challenges have made me grow personally. Life is never dull when you belong to the quilting world. Often, when I close the door late on a Sunday night, exhausted after redecorating the tables, shelves, and window displays, I look back and see my corner store glowing in the night sky. It's then that I know it really is worth it.

# Resources

## Smocking Supplies

Find smocking supplies at any shop that carries heirloom sewing supplies or contact:

Clotilde
PO Box 22312
Ft. Lauderdale, FL 33335-2312
1-800-772-2891 or 305-761-8655

Country Bumpkin
PO Box 194
Kent Town, South Australia 5071

Sally Stanley Creative Smocking
PO Box 1324
Lake Oswego, OR 97035

The Children's Corner
3814 Cleghorn Ave.
Box 150161
Nashville, TN 37215
1-800-543-6915 (Retail and wholesale)

For a colour catalogue, send $5 (U.S. or Australian currency) or your Mastercard or Visa credit card number, expiration date, and signature for airmail delivery. The catalogue includes quilt kits, bear kits, doll kits, embroidery and smocking kits, fabric packets, notions, and ribbons.

Write to:  The Calico House
2 Napoleon Street
Cottesloe 6011
Western Australia

Fax: 9-383-4437 (From the United States, dial 011-61 first, then the remaining numbers; from other countries, check with your local telephone operator.)